COMPUTER–AIDED ESTIMATING

A GUIDE TO GOOD PRACTICE

WILLIAM SHER

LONGMAN

The CHARTERED
INSTITUTE OF
BUILDING

Addison Wesley Longman Limited
Edinburgh Gate, Harlow
Essex CM20 2JE, England
and Associated Companies throughout the world

Co-published with The Chartered Institute of Building through
Englemere Services Limited
Englemere, Kings Ride, Ascot
Berkshire SL5 8BJ, England

First published 1996

British Library Cataloguing in Publication Data
A catalogue entry for this title is available from the British Library

ISBN 0-582-27324-2

Set by 4 in Ehrhardt 10/12 and Futura
Produced through Longman Malaysia, LSP

CONTENTS

COMPUTER-AIDED ESTIMATING

This book is to be returned on or before the last date
stamped below

LIST OF FIGURES AND TABLES

FOREWORD

The use of computer-aided estimating systems in the construction industry is becoming increasingly widespread but there is little independent information available on good practice and the fundamental requirements of such systems. This book highlights the main features that should be present in a CAE system, and gives guidance as to how best to use a system. There is a great variety of organisations which make use of CAE systems and there is a corresponding variety of systems on the market. The major alternatives which are available are included and their benefits and limitations identified.

The Chartered Institute's *Code of Estimating Practice* provides an authoritative guide to good practice in estimating and tendering for building works. It is acknowledged that in specific circumstances the procedures may have to be modified and accordingly four supplements to the *Code* have been produced:

- Refurbishment and Modernisation
- Design and Build
- Management Contracting
- Post Tender Use of Estimating Information

This further publication on computer-aided estimating covers another specific area requiring additional consideration, and is entirely consistent with the aims and intentions of the *Code of Estimating Practice* and its four supplements. The sixth edition of the *Code of Estimating Practice*, to be published in 1997, recognises the widespread use of computers and their effects not only during estimating but throughout the subsequent stages of the financial management of construction projects.

The information contained in this book will be of great interest to anyone studying or involved in the practice of estimating. I believe it will become essential reading for anyone considering implementing a CAE system or those reviewing their existing arrangements. It will hopefully lead in the long run to the further development of computer systems best suited to the actual requirements of the construction industry.

W A Rabbetts MCIOB
Chairman of the National Procurement Committee of the CIOB

PREFACE

The purpose of this book

Contractors have been preparing estimates with PC-based computer-aided estimating systems for many years (at least since 1976). However, very little has been written about the practical issues of using these systems. Most of what has been written either describes how these systems work or refers to their benefits. Using computer-aided estimating (CAE) systems outside a research or sales environment has not received much attention but is an area with its own set of unique considerations. For example, which of the time-honoured practices associated with preparing estimates manually (such as double checking the arithmetic involved in extending and totalling monetary amounts found) need to be retained and what new checks should be introduced? Very little guidance is available to estimators new to CAE and those trying to implement these systems for the first time are generally left on their own with only the advice of CAE salesmen as guidance.

In addition, students following construction management and quantity surveying courses have found it difficult to obtain information on this subject. Estimating textbooks generally include some reference to CAE, but specific guidance on the area is currently lacking.

The combination of these two factors prompted the writing of this book. The lack of authoritative guidance was identified by the Procurement Sub-committee of the Chartered Institute of Building, who commissioned this publication. Members of this committee provided guidance and constructive criticism throughout its production. In addition several developers of CAE software were consulted as were fellow academics and representatives from professional bodies. As such this book presents a picture of how CAE systems are used at the moment and how they could be used more effectively, and identifies areas of likely future progress.

Who is this book aimed at?

This book should be of interest to all construction estimators, whether they use CAE systems or not. Those familiar with CAE should find reassurance for the practices they have implemented. They will hopefully also be made aware of alternative approaches, as well as good and dubious CAE practice. Estimators new to CAE (or those contemplating its use) will gain an understanding of what lies in store for them.

In addition this book will be valuable to both students and lecturers on construction related degrees. Examples of project work are provided in an appendix and a brief discussion on how the use of computer systems may be integrated into the syllabus of construction studies is also given.

This book will provide a better understanding of how CAE systems are used and describe how to gain the maximum benefit from this approach to estimating. At a time when most of us are trying to increase our awareness of computer systems, this must surely be worthwhile.

Background assumed in the preparation of this book

This book has been written on the assumption that readers have a sound knowledge of the practices and procedures associated with estimating and tendering. If this is not the case, the texts listed in the bibliography at the end of the book are recommended reading. Chief amongst these is the *Code of Estimating Practice*, the authoritative reference in this field.

I have also assumed that readers are familiar with operating personal computer systems and have therefore provided no guidance on procedures for making back-ups of estimating data and so on. Those interested in this topic should consult the recommendations of their particular CAE system.

Reference to commercially available CAE systems

I have avoided making reference to specific computer packages wherever possible. Most CAE systems operate along similar lines and it has not been my intention to distinguish between the advantages and disadvantages of various computer programs. There are, naturally, considerable differences between CAE packages, with some systems performing certain operations more elegantly than others. However, these differences generally relate to the manner in which specific aspects of estimating are addressed rather than the principles of using computers to prepare estimates of construction costs. My aim has been to describe in general terms how computers may be used to help prepare construction estimates, to identify good practice and to provide guidelines for the effective use of these systems.

Layout of this book

This book describes how CAE systems may be used to prepare estimates and tenders for building projects. It is divided into chapters, each of which deals with a separate aspect of this process. Within each chapter the various operations necessary for the completion of each aspect are described. Where appropriate, alternative approaches and the pros and cons of each of these methods are described as well.

Bibliography to Preface

Bentley J I W (1990). *Construction tendering and estimating*. E & F N Spon (ISBN 0419142401).

Brook M (1993). *Estimating and tendering for construction work*. Butterworth Heinemann (ISBN 0750615311).

Buchan R D, Fleming F W and Kelly J R (1991). *Estimating for builders and quantity surveyors*. Butterworth Heinemann (ISBN 0750600411).

Chartered Institute of Building (1983). *Code of estimating practice*, 5th edition (ISBN 0906600650).

Chartered Institute of Building (1987). *Code of estimating practice: supplement no. 1 – refurbishment and modernisation*. December (ISBN 0906600952).

Chartered Institute of Building (1989). *Code of estimating practice: supplement no. 2 – design and build*. June (ISBN 0906600960).

Chartered Institute of Building (1989). *Code of estimating practice: supplement no. 3 – management contracting*. October (ISBN 1853800007).

Chartered Institute of Building (1993). *Code of estimating practice: supplement no. 4 – post tender use of estimating information*. December (ISBN 1853800635).

McCaffer R and Baldwin A N (1991). *Estimating and tendering for civil engineering works*, 2nd edition. BSP Professional (ISBN 0632029528).

Pilcher R (1994). *Project cost control in construction*, 2nd edition. Blackwell Scientific (ISBN 0632036370).

ACKNOWLEDGEMENTS

This book has had a long gestation period. I first thought of writing it in the mid-1980s when I started lecturing on a part-time basis at my old university in Johannesburg, South Africa. Before this I'd been involved in developing and installing computer-aided estimating systems for building contractors in the United Kingdom and in South Africa. The firms I dealt with ranged from 'one-man bands' to major contractors and I saw how computer-aided estimating systems were used in a wide variety of ways (some of which were very different to those intended by their developers!). These different approaches as well as the knowledge and experience accumulated by estimators over the years have not been widely publicised. Until recently, comparatively little has been written on this topic. Some books have been published in the United States, whilst the United Kingdom texts on construction computing only make passing reference to the subject. In addition, academic papers generally deal with research into specific aspects of estimating. I thus saw the need for a book that practitioners, students and lecturers could refer to which dealt with computer-aided estimating from a UK perspective.

The impetus to actually start writing came when I spoke of the need for this book at a Chartered Institute of Building Procurement Sub-committee meeting. Having admitted being a latent author, I was given the task of actually getting this book into print! I received tremendous support from the working party that was formed to assist me. In addition I pestered many of my colleagues at Loughborough University, as well as some vendors of computer-aided estimating systems. To all of them I owe thanks for their patience and constructive criticism. In particular I'd like to thank the following persons who helped by commenting on my efforts: Martin Brook, Ron Harrison, David Turner, David Borrie, Bryan Evans, Jacki Saunders, Mike Fleming, Bruce Wright, Andrew Baldwin, Tony Thorpe, Tony Appleton and Bill Rabbetts.

Thanks would not be complete without mentioning the following people with whom I have worked over the years and whose views on the subject have influenced my own: Syd Brett, Duncan Hyslop and Tony Hayzen.

LIST OF ABBREVIATIONS

ASCII	American standard code for information interchange
CAD	Computer-aided design
CAE	Computer-aided estimating
CEM	BSc Construction Engineering Management
CEP	Code of Estimating Practice (fifth edition published by the Chartered Institute of Building 1983)
CESSM3	Civil Engineering Standard Method of Measurement (third edition published by the Institution of Civil Engineers)
CICA	Construction Industry Computing Association
CIOB	Chartered Institute of Building
CITE	Construction industry trading electronically
CMQS	BSc Commercial Management and Quantity Surveying
CPA	Critical path analysis
EBQ	Electronic bills of quantities
ECI	European Construction Institute
EDI	Electronic data interchange
EDICON	Electronic data interchange in the construction industry
EDIFACT	Electronic data interchange for administration, commerce and transport
INFO-COMM	Information Communication (defunct EDI standard used in South Africa in the mid-1980s)
NVQ	National Vocational Qualification
OCR	Optical character recognition
OPC	Ordinary portland cement
RICS	Royal Institution of Chartered Surveyors
SMM	Standard method of measurement
SMM7	Standard method of measurement for building works (seventh edition published by the RICS/BEC)

CHAPTER 1

OVERVIEW OF COMPUTER-AIDED ESTIMATING SYSTEMS

1.1 SCOPE

This chapter describes the operation of computer-aided estimating (CAE) systems. The advantages of using these systems are described as well as some of the reasons sceptics give for not using CAE systems. A short section on current developments in hardware and software is also provided. The links that may be created between CAE systems and other construction applications are then briefly described. The chapter concludes with an overview of the contents of this book.

1.2 OVERVIEW

CAE systems allow estimators to prepare estimates for construction work by linking estimating data to bills of quantities. They also assist in obtaining quotations for the materials, plant and sub-contract constituents used in calculating bill item rates and allow estimators to make adjustments to estimated costs to arrive at a tender value. Most CAE systems operate along generally similar lines to those shown in Figure 1.1. This shows that the CAE process may be divided into the following areas:

- Entering bills of quantities.
- Linking items in bills of quantities to build-ups stored in an **estimating library**. (The extent to which previously stored data are used to assist in estimating the costs of new projects varies from estimator to estimator. As described in Chapter 3, some estimators make extensive use of library data, whereas others use estimating libraries mainly to record gang rates.)
- Preparing requests for quotations to be sent to materials suppliers, plant hire firms and sub-contractors.
- Estimating the costs of bill items. (Depending on the extent to which library data are used, this may involve changing and refining item build-ups according to the specific requirements of a project and/or calculating item rates from first principles.)
- Updating the costs of labour, materials, plant and sub-contract items.

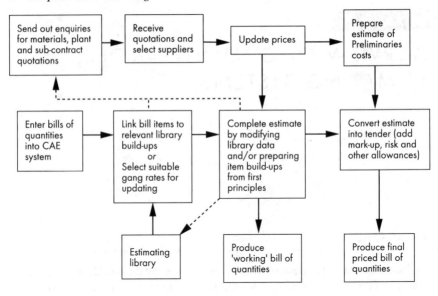

Figure 1.1   Typical layout of a computer-aided estimating system

- Preparing estimates of 'Preliminaries' costs.
- Printing out reports.
- Making adjustments and adding mark-ups to convert the estimated cost of a project into a tender sum.

The estimating procedure shown in Figure 1.1 is obviously simplified and more detailed explanations and flowcharts are provided in subsequent chapters.

It should be noted that this book deals only with CAE systems that are readily available from software vendors. It does not address 'bespoke' systems that have been developed specifically for individual organisations (though the principles described here will be equally applicable).

1.3 IMPLICATIONS OF USING COMPUTERS TO PREPARE ESTIMATES

Using a computer system to assist in estimating the cost of construction projects is not as contentious as it was in the early 1980s. Many contractors currently use them successfully on a day to day basis. This book identifies and describes in detail many of the ramifications of using these systems and a brief overview of these is given below.

- Estimators may start preparing an estimate as soon as a bill of quantities is received (i.e. they do not need to wait for quotations from suppliers and sub-contractors as these may be dealt with at a later stage of the estimating process).

- CAE systems ensure that all estimates are prepared in a consistent manner (within each estimate and between different estimates).
- They provide information that is too time consuming to produce using manual estimating methods.
- They also provide data which may be used in operations which occur once an estimate has been completed (such as cash flow predictions, interim valuation of work completed on site, and so on).

Notwithstanding these factors, CAE systems are not always seen in a positive light. Some estimators have an in-built apprehension about these systems and, according to Turner (1995), fear that 'a bill of quantities is fed in at one end and a completed estimate emerges at the other end'. This feeling of unease results in an understandable reluctance on the part of these estimators to use a system which may eventually make them redundant. However, this fear is unfounded as the vast majority of CAE systems operate as computer-**aided** systems and are not able to function unless operated by an estimator (as distinct from 'expert' and 'neural network' computer systems which incorporate varying amounts of 'computer intelligence'). Other estimators view the estimating process as too complex to be catered for by a computer system. They feel these systems inhibit their ability to use their own judgement. These concerns might have been true for some early CAE systems, but those currently on the market are extremely flexible and can be used in a wide variety of different ways which reflect the diversity of approaches used by estimators.

In some cases, those hesitant about using CAE systems are apprehensive about using computer technology generally. However, most CAE packages operate in ways that reflect manual estimating procedures. The extent to which manual methods are duplicated by CAE systems has prompted some authorities, notably Potter and Scoins (1994), to argue that this has resulted in a 'tremendous loss of opportunity' as they see that little attempt has been made to 'consider the possibility and benefits of more productive ways of producing estimates offered by the computer'. Those who feel uneasy about using CAE systems may find little comfort in these words!

Some estimators not familiar with computer systems also feel uneasy that they may lose control of the estimating process. There is no doubt that many of the tried and trusted procedures of checking manual estimates no longer apply when computer systems are used, but what checks need to be implemented to ensure that errors do not occur? This book provides some answers to this question.

1.4 LINKS TO OTHER APPLICATIONS

Figure 1.1 does not attempt to identify and explore links that may be made to other computer applications involved in the process of constructing a building. A simplified illustration of some of these links is given in Figure 1.2 (and the CIOB's fourth supplement to the *Code of Estimating Practice* (1993) deals with this topic in detail). This figure distinguishes between *technical* and *accounting* applications and shows links between computer-aided design (CAD), measurement and the production of bills of

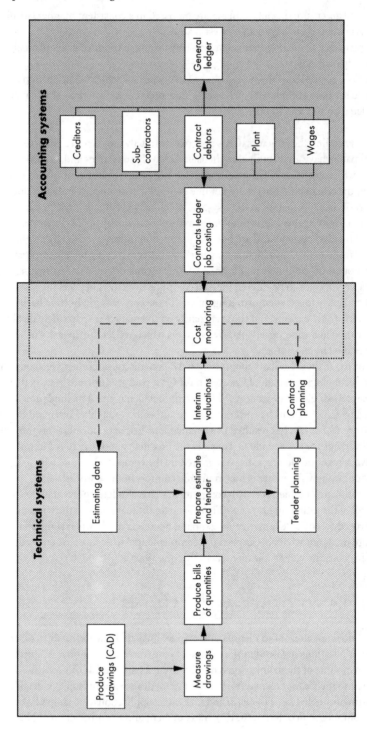

Figure 1.2   Flow chart of technical and accounting computer systems

quantities, the planning of construction operations, the production of interim claims, monitoring of costs and financial accounting. In the case of CAD, design data may be shared not only between designers (e.g. architects, structural engineers, services engineers and so on) but may also be used to generate measurements of a building. Using CAD data to produce bills of quantities in this way has been a goal to which many researchers have been working for many years. However, its application in a commercial form is still to be realised. Once bills of quantities have been prepared they may be sent to those tendering either as a traditional paper document or as electronic bills of quantities (EBQ). EBQs may be used to assist contractors to prepare estimates and tenders in a variety of ways which are described in Chapter 2. It is also possible to link estimating data to construction programs and a few computer systems provide such facilities. When links such as these are available it is usually also possible to generate forecasts of cash flow for the combination of costs and construction sequence planned. On successful bids CAE data may be used for a number of purposes, for example, as the basis of a contractors' cost monitoring system. A form of EBQ may also be used to submit interim claims for payment from contractors to clients' quantity surveyors.

Estimates provide data on which contractors' information systems depend. When stored in a computer system, specially developed programs may access this data and use it to prime other construction applications (and indeed, some vendors of construction software argue that investing in CAE systems may be justified solely in terms of benefits to applications *other* than estimating!). The importance of estimating data to these other construction operations cannot be overlooked. Although a discussion of these topics is outside the scope of this book, reference is made to these 'bolt-on' applications where they impact on the estimating function.

1.5   DEVELOPMENTS IN HARDWARE AND SOFTWARE

The rate at which computer hardware has progressed over the past two decades has been astounding. Paulson (1995) observes that 'if the economics and productivity of aircraft had evolved as rapidly as those of computers, one could travel from San Francisco to New York for just a few cents and arrive within seconds of taking off!' The relevance of these developments to the evolution of CAE systems is described below.

1.5.1   Hardware

There are several authoritative publications which refer to this topic (including Paulson's (1995) concise and up-to-date review and Stewart and Stewart's (1986) slightly older but equally relevant work). This section provides a brief overview of some of the developments in personal computer technology that motivated Paulson's remarks above.

- *Disk space*   In the early 1980s, the storage capacity of personal computers was modest. CAE systems of this vintage were constrained to the capacity of floppy disks and when fixed disks became widely used a ten megabyte disk was considered the norm. Currently a disk capacity of 500 megabytes is considered to be usual. This dramatic reduction in the cost of storage space has had a marked effect on the way computer programs are written. Effectively this abundance of disk space has removed a factor which has, until recently, constrained the development of software. A further consequence of this availability of disk space is that it is possible to store large amounts of data, and this aspect is particularly relevant where optical scanners are used in the CAE process (see 'Optical scanning' below).

- *Disk access speeds*   The speed with which computer hard disks are able to locate specific programs and data has also increased significantly over the past decade.
- *Memory*   Similarly, the amount of memory that modern computers are sold with has also increased. This has largely been due to the requirements of Microsoft's Windows[TM] environment under which many computer programs operate. The availability of large amounts of memory has, in turn, further alleviated some of the constraints that software developers needed to work under, resulting in larger, more complex and more functional programs.
- *Processor speed*   The speed with which computers are able to run programs and process data has also increased markedly. This has, in many cases, influenced the way in which computer programs are developed as there is no longer the same need to fully exploit the potential of computer processors. The speed with which the latest processors operate makes even inefficiently written programs seem fast.
- *Optical scanning*   Although many people who use computer systems in the construction industry have advocated the electronic communication of data for years, the reality is that very little progress has been made in this area over the past decade. Optical scanners are seen by some as a panacea to this problem as they provide a way of turning paper-based documents into an electronic form. It is likely that optical scanners will play an increasingly important role in producing estimates and some of the ways they are currently being used are described in Sections 2.4 and 5.3.2.

1.5.2 Software

The rapid developments in computer hardware described above have impacted significantly on the way in which programs are currently being developed. The influence of fast computer processors and large amounts of disk storage space have already been mentioned. The main result has been that the environment in which computer programs operate has become much simpler to use thanks to the likes of operating systems such as Windows. In relation to computer programs written specifically for the construction industry, the advent of Windows and other general purpose business application software (such as Microsoft Excel, Microsoft Word and so on) have raised the expectations of construction professionals and estimators alike. Using a mouse, 'pull-down' menus and so on have become accepted ways of communicating with a computer. However, upgrading software to exploit new technology and techniques is expensive, both for software developers and for end-users. The decision on when to invest in these changes is especially difficult for developers of low volume (and consequently low budget) programs such as CAE systems. Not only is there the considerable cost of redevelopment, but they also need to take into account the attitude of their existing clients, many of whom are concerned at the cost of upgrading their existing hardware

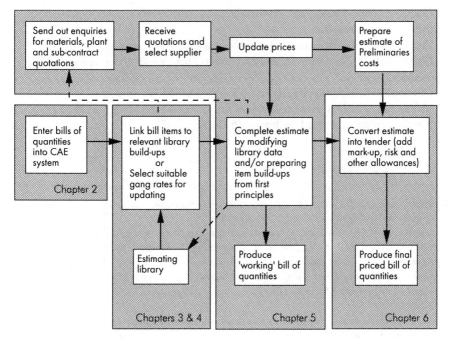

Figure 1.3   The contents of this book

and of training staff to operate new systems. Developers are therefore caught in a quandary as potential clients want the latest in technology and many existing clients are happy with the status quo. An additional factor that software vendors have to consider is that of competing software companies, all of whom are seeking to gain a marketable advantage.

In summary, recent hardware developments have made it possible for programmers to write large programs which function much more quickly than their predecessors. In addition, the availability of cheap disk storage space has made it feasible to store extremely large amounts of data and, as a consequence, optical scanners are likely to become widely used. These developments have, as yet, not been fully exploited by most CAE systems though this is likely to occur in time. Future development of hardware is likely to continue making developers' and users' decisions on when to invest in new technology even more difficult.

1.6   STRUCTURE OF THIS BOOK

Figure 1.3 provides details of the structure of this book.

- Chapter 2 deals with entering bills of quantities into CAE systems.
- Chapter 3 describes the various ways in which estimating data may be stored in estimating libraries.

- Chapter 4 provides guidelines on the coding and classification systems required when collecting estimating data.
- Chapter 5 describes the procedure of producing an estimate using a CAE system.
- Chapter 6 deals with converting an estimate into a tender and the action taken with successful bids.
- Chapter 7 deals with training estimators how to use CAE systems.
- An appendix provides an example of how the subject of computing is taught on a CIOB accredited course at Loughborough University, UK.

1.7   REFERENCES

Chartered Institute of Building (1993). *Code of estimating practice; supplement no. 4 — post tender use of estimating information.* Ascot, ISBN 1853800635.

Paulson B C Jnr (1995). *Computer applications in construction.* McGraw Hill, ISBN 007048967X.

Potter D and Scoins D (1994). 'Computer-aided estimating'. In Fayek A, Duffield C F and Young D M. A review of commercially available cost-estimating software systems for the construction industry. *Engineering Management Journal*, Vol. 6, No. 4, 4 December.

Stewart R D and Stewart A L (1986). *Microestimating for civil engineers.* McGraw Hill, ISBN 0070614636.

Turner D (1995). Consultation with D Turner (FCIOB), member of CIOB Procurement Sub-Committee, October 1995.

CHAPTER 2

ENTERING BILLS OF QUANTITIES

2.1 SCOPE

This chapter describes the various ways estimators enter bills of quantities into their estimating systems. The methods dealt with include re-typing bills, using optical scanners, and electronic bills of quantities.

2.2 INTRODUCTION

As described in Section 1.2, CAE systems allow item build-ups to be stored in a library and re-used, where appropriate, in new estimates. They also provide calculation facilities to compute bill item rates and the total cost of an estimate, as well as presentation facilities which provide a wide variety of report formats and screen displays. However elegant and sophisticated these facilities are, they are of limited value unless a bill of quantities has been entered into a CAE system. Without this the estimating process cannot begin. As most bills of quantities are prepared using a computer program of one sort or another, it would seem logical for an electronic version of a bill to be made available to those invited to tender. This rarely happens at the moment (though its occurrence is increasing). The methods of entering bills into CAE systems that contractors generally use are the following:

- Re-typing the bill items into a system.
- Using an **optical scanner** and **optical character recognition** software to prepare an electronic bill of quantities (EBQ).

2.3 RE-TYPING BILLS OF QUANTITIES

This is the simplest way of entering bill items into a CAE system. The information to be typed in includes:

- bill references (e.g. Administration Block – this may be optional with some CAE systems)
- work group/trade references (e.g. Excavations – this may also be optional)
- page numbers (e.g. page 165)
- item references (e.g. item c)
- item descriptions (e.g. Excavate top soil to be preserved, average depth 300 mm – this may also be optional)
- units of measurement (e.g. m^2)
- quantities (e.g. 143)

This approach is time consuming and prone to errors. The effort required to accomplish it has prompted estimators and software developers to devise various short-cuts. These include:

- *Library item descriptions*   The first of these exploits CAE facilities which link bill items to estimating data previously stored in an estimating library (this is described in Chapter 3). If this is done, the item descriptions stored in these libraries may be used instead of typing in item descriptions. However, this approach may cause problems as it is unlikely that library descriptions will exactly match those appearing in the bill of quantities being worked on. This in effect means that estimators will have two versions of a bill of quantities available to them (i.e. the official document and the contractor's own version with item descriptions accessed from an estimating library). The potential for discrepancies between these two documents needs to be recognised as it may cause confusion. This method should therefore be used with caution.
- *Shortened item descriptions*   A second approach involves typing in a shortened version of the full item descriptions (e.g. Facings type A in half brick wall). According to Brook (1995) this may also cause problems as 'we find that estimators are not reading the printed (original) bill when resourcing items and can miss part of the detailed description, for example, the colour of the mortar'.
- *No item descriptions*   Thirdly, some estimators choose not to re-type item descriptions at all. In this instance bill items are identified solely by their bill/page/ item reference. Obviously if this is done, continual reference needs to be made to the original bill of quantities. As this document is legally binding, proponents of this approach view the need for estimators to continually refer to it as an advantage. They argue that it avoids the possible misinterpretations and mistakes described in the first two methods.

Clearly the task of re-typing item descriptions is an onerous one. There are no instant solutions and any use of short-cuts such as those described above is likely to cause problems at a later stage of the estimating process. Furthermore, some of these short-cuts are not suitable for clerical staff to complete and having estimators perform these tasks may be an inefficient use of their time. Can any of these short cuts be used to advantage? To answer this question it is necessary to consider the uses to which CAE bills may be put. There are three main areas:

- *CAE bills as tender submissions*   In some cases bills of quantities need to be submitted at the time of tender. Estimators using CAE systems naturally want to avoid having to 'ink in' item rates and extensions into bills and submitting CAE bills is an obvious and attractive alternative. In such instances most quantity surveyors insist that the item descriptions printed out by CAE systems match those provided in the original bill of quantities. Using library item descriptions and abbreviated descriptions is thus not acceptable for this purpose (though, in certain circumstances, clients' quantity surveyors may accept CAE bills without any descriptions' according to Harrison [1995]). In these cases the short-cuts described above do not provide a solution.

- *CAE bills as requests for quotations* Sending out requests for quotations to materials suppliers, sub-contractors and the like forms a major part of the estimating process and is an area which most CAE systems address (Section 5.3 describes these request for quotations sub-systems). Where these systems are used, item descriptions need to be complete and accurate. As before, library item descriptions and abbreviated descriptions are not acceptable in this instance as suppliers need to know exactly what they are to provide.

- *CAE bills used solely in estimating department* According to Brook (1995), most estimators currently involved in preparing estimates for building work do not use CAE bills of quantities for their tender submission or as part of their requests for quotations. When bills are used purely as internal working documents the use of abbreviated item descriptions or simply having bill/page/item references (as described above) is viable.

The method of entering/re-typing item descriptions selected is thus influenced by the uses to which CAE bills are put. In summary, where these documents are to be legally binding, they need to be exact replicas of the original bill of quantities.

Table 2.1 highlights some important considerations relating to the entry of bills of quantities into a CAE system.

2.4 USING AN OPTICAL SCANNER TO PREPARE AN ELECTRONIC BILL

Since the mid-1980s, some estimators have used optical scanners to transform paper-based bills of quantities into an electronic form. Two approaches have evolved, namely optical character recognition (OCR) and providing an image of each bill page.

2.4.1 Optical character recognition (OCR) bills of quantities

These systems allow the text on pages of a paper-based bill to be transformed into an electronic form. To do this, each page of a bill needs to be passed through an optical scanner. This device takes an electronic 'picture' of a page and optical character recognition (OCR) software is then used to translate these pictures into alphabetic characters and numbers. The resulting electronic bill of quantities (EBQ) then needs to be entered into a CAE system. To achieve this many of these systems frequently provide

Table 2.1   Summary of important considerations relating to the entry of bills of quantities into a CAE system

Requirements	Notes	Good practice
It is essential that bill item quantities are **accurately** entered into a CAE system.	Check that: – all items have been entered – all item quantities are correct – all units of measurement are correctly entered	Check that bill item quantities have been correctly entered by comparing the client's bill with CAE print-outs. This is best done by one person reading out item quantities and another ticking them off. Alternatively: – Manually total all item quantities in the client's bill. This total should be the same as that calculated for the CAE bill (some CAE systems provide this 'checksum' total). *Do not* submit tender unless these numbers can be reconciled. (If this check is done on a page-by-page basis, the potential for compensating errors to occur is reduced.) – Check that the correct number of items have been entered for each page. It is possible for compensating errors to go undetected unless this final check is made.
Avoid conflict between clients' bills and CAE bills. This may occur where: – item descriptions have been transferred from an estimating library (it is likely that these descriptions will be worded differently from clients' bills of quantities) – abbreviated item descriptions have been entered into the CAE system	– Some clients' quantity surveyors may accept CAE bills without item descriptions. – Estimators need to be certain they are working on the correct item.	When using a CAE system estimators should refer to the original printed bill, as this is the document to which construction contractors are legally bound.
Staff motivation	Re-typing bills of quantities is tedious. A never ending set of bills to enter is likely to cause staff to lose motivation and work inaccurately.	Where possible: – Use a range of input methods to capture bills of quantities. Re-typing should be used as a last resort. – Vary the work of those entering bills of quantities to incorporate other activities.
Provide the CAE bill of quantities **in time**	Re-typing bills of quantities is time consuming and adequate provision needs to be made for it to occur.	Where this method is used, start typing the bill in as soon as possible.

'import' facilities which translate EBQs into the format required by the CAE system concerned (this procedure is similar to that described in Section 2.5 below).

Two factors have prevented this method of entering bill data into CAE systems from becoming popular. The first is cost. When introduced, scanning hardware and software cost two to two-and-a-half times as much as a typical CAE installation. This made it uneconomical for small to medium sized contractors (though some used computer bureaux to scan documents). More recently the cost of these items has reduced significantly and this is now less likely to be considered prohibitively expensive.

The second factor is the accuracy of scanned documents as they are rarely without error. Referring to the accuracy obtained by the scanning technology available in the late 1980s, Barton (1991) describes the situation in this way: '90% accuracy was a typical working figure, although this depended on the quality of the original document. The time taken in searching for the 10% inaccurate items often took as long as entering the text manually'.

Although these systems have improved, accuracy and the effort required to rectify errors remains an issue. Harrison (1995) states that: 'whilst it is possible to obtain 99% accuracy with many bills, most errors will be in alphabetic characters and will probably not affect the sense of what is produced. However, some errors will be in numbers with quantities in some cases being completely omitted for no obvious reason.'

These comments, Harrison continues, refer to bills that 'lend' themselves to scanning (i.e. those prepared using word processing or similar software that produce text in a consistent way). However, many bills do not satisfy these requirements. Headings which stray outside description columns, measured items without item numbers, headings with item numbers, pages of varying length, unusual fonts and so on can make a bill more difficult to interpret. Whilst most bills will respond to the use of this technology, the extent of manual checking and editing necessary can be very time consuming. Even with good bills, according to Harrison, the scanning process including checking and editing is unlikely to be faster than 20–30 pages per hour and may be much slower.

As a consequence of both of these factors, OCR bills have received a luke-warm response from those estimators who have used them.

2.4.2 'Imaged' bills of quantities

The inaccuracy of OCR bills has prompted some developers of CAE software to use optically scanned images of bill pages in their systems. This process (called 'imaging') is equivalent to pasting a picture of a complete bill page in a CAE system and avoids having to use OCR software, thus obviating the problems of correctly interpreting alphabetic characters and numbers. However, imaging has the following drawbacks:

- A certain amount of data still needs to be entered manually (e.g. bill/trade/page/item reference, units of measurement, quantity and so on. See Figure 2.1).
- Imaging a bill of quantities uses considerable computer disk space. As already mentioned in Section 1.5.1, the cost of disk storage space has fallen significantly in recent years. If, however, existing hardware needs to be purchased or upgraded, these costs will need to be weighed against the benefits of this method.

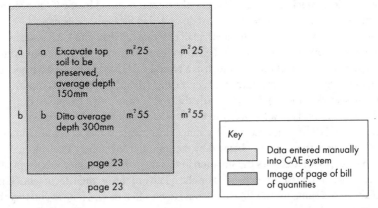

Figure 2.1   Example of data stored in a CAE system where optically scanned images of bill pages are used to provide bill data

The main advantage of this approach is that it produces CAE bills of quantities which are a near-perfect replica of those provided by clients' quantity surveyors. A simplified representation of the way in which CAE systems store imaged bills is illustrated in Figure 2.1.

In summary, **OCR bills of quantities** require comprehensive checking to ensure they provide an accurate representation of original documentation. **Imaged bills** by-pass this problem but in so doing require some data to be entered into a CAE system. The relative advantages and disadvantages of these two methods again need to be weighed up against the intended use of these documents. OCR and imaged bills are usually used where data produced by estimators' computer systems are to be provided in tender submissions or in a 'request for quotations' sub-system (See Section 5.3). Where these bills are intended purely for in-house use, it is unlikely that this will justify their cost. The use of optical scanners described here is an interim solution to the problem and the next section in this chapter describes a more effective solution.

Table 2.2 highlights some important considerations relating to scanned bills of quantities.

2.5   OBTAINING ELECTRONIC BILLS FROM CLIENTS' QUANTITY SURVEYORS

Estimators have been exploring ways of avoiding re-typing bills of quantities into CAE systems ever since these systems were invented. One approach that has been a dream of estimators for many years is to obtain bills in a 'computer-friendly' format that can be fed directly into their CAE systems. For example, in the 1960s Alvey (1976) foresaw a time when paper tapes containing bills of quantities data would be passed from quantity surveyors to contractors. Developments in computer technology have overtaken the medium of communication that Alvey proposed, but the transfer of bills between quantity surveyors and construction contractors is still far from widespread.

Table 2.2   Summary of important considerations relating to optically scanned bills of quantities

Requirements	Notes	Good practice
Accuracy	– When *OCR bills* are used, accuracy can only be obtained if time and effort are deployed as well. These systems do not provide a completely automated solution. – *Imaged bills* are not immune to errors as item quantities need to be entered manually.	Good practice associated with manual entry of bill data is described in Table 2.1.
Cost	The benefits of using optical scanners and related software need to be weighed against the costs of using these systems.	To operate these systems efficiently, sheet feeders (attachments that allow scanners to stack several pages for scanning) need to be used.

2.5.1   Requirements of EBQs

This concept of transferring bills of quantities between clients' quantity surveyors and contractors' estimators recognises the fact that bills of quantities are in most cases compiled using a computer system. It seeks to have these 'computer versions' of bills made available to contractors so that they can be used to prime CAE systems. However, many issues are involved when exchanging data electronically between these parties.

With regard to **software**:

- Computer-aided systems used to produce bills of quantities (which range from general purpose word processing systems to dedicated bills production systems) need to incorporate facilities which prepare bills of quantities in an electronic form.
- The electronic documents so created need to be in a form that can be interpreted by contractors' CAE systems.
- These CAE systems need to have facilities for receiving this data.
- Bills of quantities priced using CAE systems ideally need to be able to be transferred back to quantity surveyors' systems. (Some quantity surveyors at the forefront of these developments already request that contractors return these electronic documents to them with their tender so that analyses of different tenders can be performed.)

As far as **hardware** is concerned:

- If data is to be exchanged by means of computer disks, these should be of a format compatible with the hardware used by the parties concerned.
- If exchange is to take place via a computer network, appropriate communications hardware (and software) needs to be available to both the sender and receiver.

To date some quantity surveyors have been hesitant to provide bills of quantities in an electronic format. The reasons for this reluctance include:

- concerns about the legal validity of electronic documents
- the belief that contractors have no need for them
- lack of facilities of their software for the purposes of transferring data
- the lack of computer expertise to produce them

Legally the issue is clear – EBQs do not replace printed bills and probably will not do so for some time to come. (More information on legal issues surrounding EDI in the construction industry may be found in a recent ECI [1994] document.) Thus, in the case of a discrepancy between the item quantity for a particular item as presented in a paper document and that contained in the EBQ for the same project, the figure included in the paper-based document is the legally binding one. This principle is well established – Comninos (1987) stated in a paper delivered in 1987 that EBQs did: '. . . not . . . (replace) the normal tender documentation which will still constitute the legal bill of quantities and bid. Its primary function is to speed up the estimating cycle and to allow for a uniform bill of quantities in digital form which can be used by the contractor for estimating and by the client for his own analyses.'

2.5.2   Reasons why EBQs are not made readily available

- EBQs have not, until recently, been requested by contractors. This situation is changing but it is no wonder that clients' quantity surveyors see little urgency in providing electronic documents for which there is, at best, scant demand.
- Lack of familiarity with computer systems may also inhibit the production of EBQs. Quantity surveyors are not alone in needing to address this issue. There is no instant solution to this problem and it is only likely to be resolved with the passage of time.
- Quantity surveyors may see no benefit to themselves in providing EBQs. Preparing bills of quantities generally occurs within a stringent timeframe and having to complete an additional task (largely for the benefit of tenderers) could be seen as not worth the effort (See also Section 2.6).

Some bills of quantities *are* currently being transferred electronically between clients' quantity surveyors and contractors. A few quantity surveyors provide disks containing 'ASCII' or 'text' files of bills of quantities with the paper-based bills. These EBQs are generated by the software normally used to prepare bills of quantities (most of which incorporates such conversion facilities). However, estimators who wish to use these electronic bills in their CAE systems are not able to do so without first having to manipulate the EBQ data. This involves transferring the data provided in the EBQ to appropriate areas of their CAE system. A simplified version of this process is illustrated in Figure 2.2.

This transfer of data is relatively simple to accomplish where all bills of quantities are presented in exactly the same way. However, there is little consistency in the manner in which different quantity surveyors lay out their bills of quantities. For example, some present **item quantities** before **units of measurement** and so on. These seemingly trivial differences need to be catered for if the data in an EBQ are to be used in a CAE system. To overcome these issues and to simplify the transfer process, many CAE systems provide 'import' programs which accommodate the variety of forms of

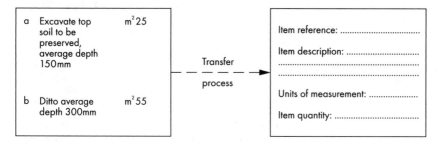

Electronic bill of quantities (ASCII/Text format)   Format of data required by CAE system

Figure 2.2   The transfer process that needs to occur before EBQs can be used in CAE systems

presentation EBQs are produced in and transform these into a format required by the CAE system being used.

EBQs of the type described above are clearly only an interim step along the way to transporting bills of quantities electronically. The transfer process illustrated in Figure 2.2 is an unnecessary step as it is technically possible for quantity surveyors to produce bills which are directly intelligible to contractors' CAE systems. The means to achieving this are, seemingly, straightforward. Quantity surveyors and estimators need to agree on a format that EBQs will be presented in and, once this is done, the developers of bill production and CAE software will adapt their systems to transfer and receive data in this standard format. However, the path to this idyllic situation has so far been tortuous. A standard for transferring data in this way exists in the form of EDIFACT (a résumé of recent developments in this area is given by Thorpe et al [1994]). EDIFACT is an exchange standard which has been adopted by the European Union, the United Nations, EDIBUILD (the European construction industry EDI group) and the American National Standards Institute (ANSI) and is already widely used by many industries. In the early 1990s a UK body called EDICON (Electronic Data Interchange in the Construction Industry) was set up to 'increase the business efficiency . . . through improvements in the communications of the (construction) industry as a whole'. To achieve this EDICON has promoted the adaptation of the EDIFACT standard to meet the requirements of the construction industry. However, the resulting EDIFACT messages have so far not gained the wide acceptance from quantity surveyors and estimators necessary to assure its success. EDIFACT is far sighted in that it provides a framework for communication that extends beyond that required for transferring bills of quantities between quantity surveyors and contractors. As such it provides more than these parties need at a time when some are not convinced they need anything at all! (It is interesting to contrast this situation with that experienced in South Africa in the mid-1980s where attempts made to implement a similar standard (called INFO-COMM) also failed. In this case the standard agreed to was too restrictive and was rapidly overtaken by developments in computer technology.)

More recently twenty construction companies – including contractors, materials suppliers and quantity surveyors – have formed a body called CITE (Construction Industry Trading Electronically) to promote electronic interchange of data (EDI)

Table 2.3   Summary of important considerations relating to the provision of EBQs by clients' quantity surveyors

Requirements	Notes	Good practice
A **reliable** and **workable** method by which electronic bills of quantities can be made available by clients' quantity surveyors to contractors' estimators and vice versa.	– Computer systems to achieve this are available (and have been for some time). – There is some reluctance on the part of both clients' and quantity surveyors and contractors' estimators to adopt this approach.	A widely accepted standard for defining the layout of bills of quantities for electronic transfer is desirable. To gain this acceptance a standard needs to address the requirements of all parties using these documents (i.e. clients' quantity surveyors, contractors' estimators, sub-contractors and materials suppliers).

between construction companies. The problem CITE members identified is the fact that, as few people are currently using EDI, there is no incentive to try it. MacNeil (1995) notes that this has been likened to the use of telephones in the following way: 'If you're the only one with it, it's useless. If there are only two, it's not much better. But if everyone has one, it's invaluable.'

To help ensure that they are successful, CITE have initially restricted the scope of their approach to transmitting bills of quantities from quantity surveyors to contractors and invoices from suppliers to contractors. It is noteworthy that the standard suggested for transferring bills of quantities is an ASCII file. This reflects a pragmatic approach because, as has already been mentioned, the computer programs that many clients' quantity surveyors use are able to produce ASCII files and most CAE systems already provide facilities to receive such files.

It remains to be seen whether CITE will be more successful than EDICON in promoting the electronic exchange of bills of quantities. Should this attempt fail, there is a possibility that the benefits of EDI are likely to remain lost to the construction industry for an even longer period. The conservative attitude of contractors is widely recognised and the failure of another attempt to implement EDI may well harden attitudes. There is then a likelihood that construction estimators may have a standard imposed on them by other parties (e.g. client's quantity surveyors).

Table 2.3 summarises considerations relating to EBQs provided by the client's quantity surveyor.

2.6   'PROGRAMMED' EBQS

Another approach sometimes adopted by a few engineers, quantity surveyors and clients is for bills of quantities *and computer programs* to be sent to contractors on disk. The programs are supplied to enable tenderers to read the bills on their computer systems and also so that rates can be entered onto the disk for each bill item. Tenderers are required to return their priced disks so that the bills of quantities of all those tendering may be compared and analysed. This approach has obvious benefits for clients' representatives but none for contractors. It provides no assistance to them in entering bill items into their computer systems (as the programs provided do not make it possible for items contained on the disk to be exported to CAE systems, or for the rates prepared by CAE systems to be fed back to the disk) and it creates extra work as rates have to be manually entered onto the disk for each item. It is therefore not surprising that, according to Harrison (1995), some tenderers have simply refused to enter the rates as required.

2.7 BENEFITS AND CHALLENGES OF EBQS

Entering item rates in 'programmed' EBQs is an onerous task and contractors see no benefit to themselves in assisting quantity surveyors to analyse the bills of those submitting tenders. In a similar vein, it has already been mentioned (in Section 2.5.2) that quantity surveyors may feel that providing EBQs to contractors is nothing but an extra task for them to complete. Clearly the interests of both quantity surveyors and contractors need to be addressed if EBQs are to become widely used. Most of the technical problems associated with transferring bills electronically between quantity surveyors and contractors have been addressed. It is therefore largely an issue of convincing sufficient parties to participate.

However, one area which still requires a solution is where bills of quantities are altered during the tender period. It is inevitable that changes to some bills will be made either by adding and/or omitting items, and/or by changing item quantities and so on. Many quantity surveyors' bill production systems automatically allocate references to each item, and making these changes thus impacts on the numbering of other bill items. The consequences of these alterations are severe where a bill has already been imported into a contractor's CAE system. In such cases items will have been stored with their original item references and any changes to these will invalidate the data stored in contractors' systems. These data may include item build-ups, lists of sub-contract items and so on. Harrison (1995) notes that: 'In general it is easier and safer to make changes manually and individually'.

This is one of the most challenging technical issues remaining to be solved at this stage. According to Cole (1995), the CITE initiative recognises this requirement and provides an appropriate solution to it.

2.8 SUMMARY

In summary, the advantages of EBQs and to a lesser extent, OCR and imaged bills, are clear and tangible. Those contractors that have used them successfully are positive about them. The lack of availability of EBQs cannot be blamed solely on clients' quantity surveyors. Until contractors call for electronic documents on a regular basis, their use will be reserved for those contractors who have geared their estimating practices to exploit them.

2.9 REFERENCES

Alvey R J (1976). *Computers in Quantity Surveying*. Macmillan.

Barton P (1991). Developments in computer aided estimating systems. *NICMAR Journal of Construction Management*, Vol. VI, No. II, July. ISSN 0970–3675.

Brook M (1995). Consultation with M Brook (FCIOB), Deputy Chairman, Procurement Committee, Chartered Institute of Building, September 1995.

Cole T (1995). Consultation with T Cole, Managing Director, Interlock (Project Manager for CITE), October 1995.

Comninos D (1987). Data exchange. At 'Gaining the competitive edge' Quantity Surveying Conference, Rosebank Hotel, Johannesburg, South Africa, May 1987.

EDICON Membership Prospectus.

European Construction Institute (1994). *Data transfer and EDI. Vol. 1 An Introduction*. ISBN 1873844263

Harrison R (1995). Consultation with R Harrison (FCIOB), Managing Director, Manifest Systems Ltd, September 1995.

MacNeil J (1995). Transfer Deal. *Building*, 13 April.

Thorpe A, Baldwin A N and Lewis T (1994). Recent developments in EDI for construction project cycle information. Paper presented to the Society for Computer Integrated Buildings, Washington, USA, June 1994.

CHAPTER 3

ESTIMATING 'LIBRARIES'

3.1 SCOPE

This chapter deals with the various ways estimators use previously stored estimating data to assist in the preparation of estimates based on bills of quantities. The ways in which these data may be structured are identified and described, as are the ways in which these data are built up into item rates.

3.2 INTRODUCTION

In the early 1980s McCaffer and Sher (1981) identified the abilities of computer systems to act as **calculators, report writers** and **filing systems** as being of central importance when computer systems are used to assist in estimating the costs of construction projects. Since then CAE systems have been developed to exploit these aspects and have matured from academic research projects into tried and trusted computer systems. Two distinct approaches have evolved over the past decade. The first takes advantage of the ability to store (or file) data. With this approach, labour, plant, materials, sub-contract costs as well as associated gang rates and item build-ups are stored in an **estimating library** (see Figure 1.1). These data are then re-used to assist in producing the cost of new estimates. Estimating libraries are time consuming to develop as labour, plant, materials and sub-contract prices as well as item build-ups appropriate to a wide range of conditions need to be collected. These data need to be carefully structured so that specific data can be found when they are needed. The effort required to accumulate sufficient data in a logical way has discouraged some estimators and has led to a second approach which concentrates more on using CAE systems as calculators. Proponents of this method see the effort of establishing and maintaining an estimating library as outweighing the benefits of re-using these data. These systems thus serve as sophisticated calculators which perform estimating calculations in a manner suited and familiar to estimators.

However, distinguishing between these two approaches is artificial as all CAE systems provide calculation facilities and most provide storage facilities in the form of estimating libraries. The importance of this distinction is that estimators use these systems in many and varied ways. This chapter deals first of all with estimating libraries and then with the calculations facilities provided with CAE systems. The different approaches of estimators are highlighted throughout.

3.3 'RESOURCE BASED' LIBRARIES

The manner in which estimating data are structured is obviously dependent upon the estimating technique used (i.e. unit rate, operational rate and so on) and the particular CAE system used. The structure that has gained widest acceptance amongst developers of this software and estimators is the **resource based** approach. This method differentiates between data that change regularly (for example, the **costs** of labour, materials, plant and sub-contract resources, which are all likely to differ from project to project) and that which is more stable (for example, the **rate** at which certain of these resources are likely to perform or be used in a given set of circumstances. These will probably remain constant for those conditions).

Generally, resource based CAE systems use two broad categories of data (see Figure 3.1) where the volatile components (called **resources** or **components** in different CAE systems) are stored separately from the more stable bill items (called **items, work groups, composites, clusters, op codes, activities** or **elements**). In this book the terms resource and item are used.

The resource based approach may be used with both unit rate and operational rate estimating. It is ideally suited to unit rate estimating and is also frequently adopted by those CAE systems which provide operational estimating facilities.

The underlying principle of this approach is that costs are only stored for resources and that item costs are derived from them (i.e. the cost of an item is calculated by

```
LABOUR RESOURCES
Bricklayer    £7.50/hr
Labourer      £5.50/hr

MATERIAL RESOURCES
Bricks        £200.00/thou
Cement        £5.00/50 kg
Sand          £6.50/tonne
```

Volatile data
This data is likely to change from project to project. It is generally quick and easy to alter.

```
ITEMS
Half brick wall (per m²)
60 bricks
0.022 m³ mortar
1.4  brickwork gang hours
     (gang made up of one
     bricklayer hour and half
     labourer hour)
```

Relatively stable data
The time it takes to do a specific item of work is generally taken to be the same from project to project. The cost of each item is calculated by referring to the latest resource data.

Figure 3.1   The resource based approach to computer-aided estimating

multiplying the cost of each constituent resource by its requirement and totalling these amounts for all resources). The main advantage of this method is that it simplifies updating the costs of items. To appreciate this, consider a resource such as cement, a material which is used in many construction operations (for example, concrete work, brickwork, plastering, roofing and so on). In most bills of quantities, the items that are likely to incorporate cement will probably be numerous. With this approach, the price of cement is stored once and used many times. By changing the cost of cement, the costs of all items containing this resource are automatically updated. This provides a clear benefit to estimators as the effort required to re-calculate item rates using manual estimating methods is considerable. Indeed, many estimators identify this ability to revise resource costs as one of the most important advantages of using a CAE system.

By way of contrast some single file CAE systems do exist. These systems store item descriptions and rates within the same file and consequently all the benefits of updating resource costs as described above are lost. Not surprisingly these are rarely used by construction contractors and are generally sold as a supplementary part of other construction application software such as programs for preparing bills of quantities and CAD systems.

As already mentioned, where estimators use a library to store estimating data, they re-use resources and item build-ups in estimates of new projects. Two different approaches to using this data may be adopted and these are described below. Few estimators use their system in exactly the same way as their colleagues and the methods described should therefore be considered as extremes of the ways in which CAE libraries may be used. Estimators may well use a combination of these approaches to suit their own particular circumstances.

- Firstly, estimators may link the items found in a bill of quantities to relevant build-ups stored in their library. Figure 3.2 shows an estimating library which is used as a source of data for several estimates (Estimate 1, 2 and so on). This approach requires a comprehensive set of data to be accumulated (a task which is usually completed over an extended period of time). With these data available, estimates may be produced by estimators matching library data to bill items. However, even with a comprehensive estimating library, it may be difficult to find data that exactly match those found in all new tenders. In this situation estimators frequently select the closest matching library item and make minor changes to reflect the particular requirements of the estimate they are working on.
- The second approach relies less on collecting a comprehensive estimating library. Here estimators compile a set of frequently used resources and items and rely on the 'resource based' structure described above to update prices and gang rates. These are for such things as all-in rates of labour, labour gangs (e.g. a bricklaying gang consisting of two bricklayers assisted by a labourer), mortar mixes, concrete mixes and so on. With this method libraries contain far fewer entries than the first approach described above. Data may thus be collected and maintained with less effort and over a shorter period of time and, as the list is shorter, items are likely to be easier to locate as well. However, more items do need to be built up from first principles during the course of preparing an estimate. Estimators who use this method argue that once

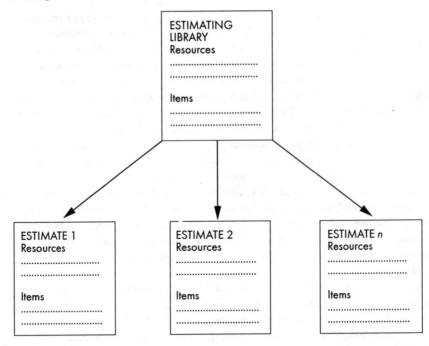

Figure 3.2   Flow of data from an estimating library to estimates

gang rates have been revised, the effort required to build up item rates is greatly reduced. In addition most estimates for building projects in the United Kingdom are currently based on sub-contractor quotations. As new quotations are obtained for each estimate (see Section 5.3), it is argued that minimal benefit is to be derived from storing this data in an estimating library. Notwithstanding this estimators do, in some cases, use their own library data to calculate the cost of sub-contract packages. These costs are then compared with sub-contract quotations to assess how competitively they have been priced. In these circumstances, a case may still be made for storing data in an estimating library.

The arrangement shown in Figure 3.2 is convenient if the data accumulated in an estimating library caters for most of the bill items found in new tenders. It takes time and effort to develop a library, and the following section highlights some of the different ways in which this may be achieved.

3.3.1   Developing a library from first principles

Where CAE libraries are developed from first principles, several aspects require attention:

- Estimators need to familiarise themselves with their CAE system before they start collecting data. This is true for all the methods described here but it is especially relevant where resources and items are to be built up for the first time. Adequate time needs to be allowed so that those operating a CAE system can become accustomed to it. It is only after using a system for a period that an appreciation of a system's full potential is developed and this understanding, in turn, influences the way in which data are arranged and collected. If work on assembling an estimating library is started before those using a system fully understand it, it is highly likely that, after a period, more efficient ways of structuring and assembling data will be devised. In such circumstances estimators will inevitably follow the precedent set by other sections of the construction industry by scrapping what they have done and starting again, hopefully getting it right the second time round!

The need to learn how a system operates should not be used as an excuse for delaying the development of a library. If this is postponed until 'some more convenient time' it will inevitably take on lesser importance than more pressing tasks, and estimators will end up not benefiting from this aspect of CAE.

- Where no estimating data have been collected, there is also a danger that insufficient thought will be given to the way in which data are structured. According to Harrison (1995): 'The library structure is probably the most important aspect of developing a library. Deciding on an approach and implementing it should be an early priority.' A framework for storing resources and items (and other data such as suppliers, sub-contractors and so on) needs to be developed so that as more and more data are stored over time they may be found again when required. This aspect is dealt with in detail in Chapter 4.

- Those responsible for the management of a construction company need to have an understanding of the tasks involved in developing a library and be committed to the expenditure involved. Costs (in the form of staff time) are likely to be significant and the benefits of using such a library are unlikely to become apparent until a meaningful amount of data has been collected.

3.3.2   Using estimate data to develop a library

Where estimators decide to develop their own libraries, many make use of data they have collected for live estimates (e.g. Estimates 1, 2 and so on as shown in Figure 3.2). It may be inconvenient to refer to several sources of data during the preparation of an estimate. To facilitate this, selected data may be transferred from previously completed estimates into a 'central' estimating library. This central library (illustrated in Figure 3.3) then forms the basis for future estimates.

The need for well thought out coding systems for both resources and items is obvious in this situation. If data are arranged haphazardly, it is only a matter of time before items and resources become difficult to locate. In addition, these coding systems will avoid unnecessary duplication of data as CAE systems warn estimators if data, for example, transferred from Tender 1 to a central library, is to be over-written by similar data from Tender 2. Some CAE systems require this estimate data to be **re-entered** in a library (i.e. they do not provide facilities for transferring data between these locations). As already mentioned, care and preparation need to be exercised in arranging these data in a logical way. Whilst having to re-enter data might seem an extreme measure, it does emphasise the need for well thought out classifications and coding systems as these are

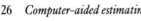

Figure 3.3   Live estimates accessing completed estimates

essential if data is to be stored in a systematic way. This aspect is dealt with in further detail in Chapter 4.

3.3.3   Purchasing library data

Most vendors of CAE systems supply estimating data. These range from basic libraries (which provide outline data for estimators to expand on and refine) to those which are extremely comprehensive. At the moment the extent to which these sources are used is difficult to determine but some points are worth noting. Firstly, it may be easier to use existing data as a starting point in developing a library than beginning from first principles. There are two main reasons for this:

- These libraries provide a framework within which additional data may be stored and/ or superfluous data deleted (this is especially true of resources).
- It may be easier to amend some production rates, wastage factors and so on than it is

to build up item rates from first principles. However, those attempting to do this should be wary. The rationale used to develop gang and item data is not always apparent from screen displays or print-outs (and is seldom documented elsewhere). Those wishing to add to existing item data may spend a substantial amount of time trying to uncover, for example, where wastage has been added to materials, if labour to off-load materials has been included, and so on. In addition, most estimators are critical of the ways their peers build up item rates and this approach to collecting item data may fail due to this reason alone.

Secondly, comments from estimators indicate that data prepared by third parties are mainly used for reference purposes (i.e. to provide guidance when unusual items are encountered). Such data are not relied upon to estimate the costs of complete bills of quantities. However, these comments may apply only to larger and medium sized contractors (as these were the ones consulted). Small contractors may well find commercially available data useful as a basis for their estimates and tenders.

3.4 MULTIPLE RESOURCE BASED LIBRARIES

Some CAE systems extend the library/estimate concept illustrated in Figure 3.2 by providing for multiple libraries. The arrangement in Figure 3.4 shows several sets of resources (catering, for example, for costs peculiar to different geographical regions), and several sets of items (for example, for different types of construction such as civil engineering work, building work, plumbing, electrical work and so on). The benefits of this approach are the following:

- The estimating data held in each part of these multiple libraries is reserved for different types of construction work. This makes it easier to locate specific data than the alternative of storing all data in the same library.
- Resources and items may be merged in various combinations to provide data suitable to the unique requirements of specific estimates (e.g. 'Midlands' resources may be combined with 'Building' items for a shopping complex in Nottingham and so on).

These benefits are generally only realised by large contractors who operate in several different geographical regions. Some may argue that many small to medium sized organisations find the task of assembling a single library demanding, and that facilities such as these are irrelevant to them. The extent to which this is true depends on each organisation. Not only do companies differ in their approach to estimating but the ways in which estimators work vary from individual to individual (even within the same company). In addition, the familiarity of estimators with the operation of their computer system also contributes to the way in which these systems are used.

These factors, combined with the fact that estimators frequently use their systems in different ways to those anticipated by their developers, make it advisable to invest in systems that are appropriate and flexible. Many of the options and facilities that are demonstrated by salesmen appear superfluous to first time users. Their application may only become apparent after a system has been used for some time. In fact, some options

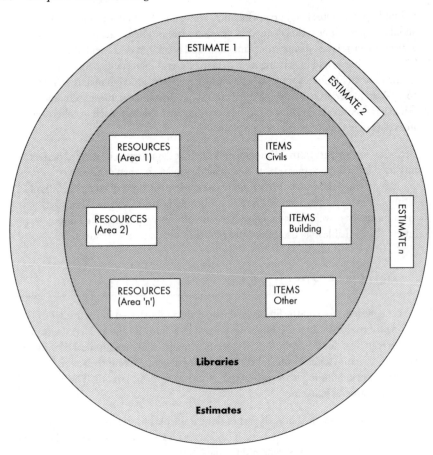

ESTIMATE 1

ESTIMATE 2

ESTIMATE n

RESOURCES
(Area 1)

ITEMS
Civils

RESOURCES
(Area 2)

ITEMS
Building

RESOURCES
(Area 'n')

ITEMS
Other

Libraries

Estimates

Figure 3.4   Arrangement of multiple sets of items and resources

may never be used because most commercially available computer systems provide
general solutions which cater for a wide variety of scenarios. The facilities used by a
particular user are likely to be a sub-set of the whole (a situation widely experienced in
the computer industry where, according to Cole (1995), 80 per cent of computer users
only employ twenty per cent of the facilities provided by packaged software). The ability
to create multiple libraries may thus appear a luxury at first. Whether or not this is so
clearly depends on many factors.

   Multiple libraries have their problems and this arrangement should not be
implemented without considering the implications of maintaining these data. To mix
and match resources and items as shown in Figure 3.4, all sets of resources need to be
arranged in an identical manner. In other words, each resource file needs to include
labour, plant, materials and sub-contract resources which have the same resource codes,
descriptions and units of measurement. This would not be an onerous requirement if
libraries remained static but this is rarely the case as most are continually being added to
and refined. Making these changes in a structured way is exacting when single sets of

resources and items are used. If multiple sets are used, this task becomes even more onerous as all changes (for example, adding a new resource or revising a production rate based on feedback from site) need to be made to *each* set of data.

In summary, there are many different ways in which libraries can be used to assist in preparing estimates. One approach is to assemble comprehensive files of estimating data. With this method, one of the main problems encountered is likely to be the effort required to assemble the data (which needs to be consistently classified and coded as described in Chapter 4). Some estimators question the benefits of collecting so much data in a library. However, many other estimators have successfully done so and use their system effectively on a day to day basis. Another approach to the use of estimating libraries is to store smaller amounts of data relating to essential resources and gang build-ups. Advocates of this approach argue that the variability of building projects makes it impossible to cater for the multitude of different bill items that may occur. Furthermore the fact that so much work on building projects in the United Kingdom is currently completed by sub-contractors makes it unnecessary, in these estimators' views, to store data relating to these operations. However, this approach does require many items to be built up from first principles during the course of an estimate. Where staff are inexperienced, this can be more time consuming than calculating item rates manually. This aspect is discussed further in Section 5.2.2.

Whatever approach is adopted, there is little difference between the library facilities provided by different CAE systems. The various methods of storing data described above reflect the individuality and imagination of estimators in applying standard CAE facilities to their particular situation.

3.5 'BUILDING BLOCKS' FOR UNIT RATE ESTIMATING

Unit rate estimating is the most popular method of calculating rates for building estimates. Item build-ups may be assembled in a number of different ways. Naturally different systems use different approaches but most make use of resources and gangs as building blocks. These are described below.

3.5.1 Resources

Resources are usually considered to be the smallest priceable component of an estimate. With building estimates they are generally classified into labour, plant, materials and sub-contract categories (civil engineering resources are sometimes classified differently). This makes it possible for the costs and quantities of similar resources to be calculated either for a particular bill item, or for a range of items. Such information is valuable for two reasons:

- It allows estimators to consider the total resource requirement of a particular building operation (e.g. 100 days of bricklayer work in foundations).
- Those adjudicating an estimate require data to be analysed in this way so that they may assess the risk attributable to each resource category.

Table 3.1   Facilities provided with resources

Facility	Explanation
Discounts	Suppliers frequently provide quotations which include discounts that depend on certain conditions (e.g. payment in 30 days). In some circumstances multiple discounts are quoted (e.g. less 5%, less 2.5%). These facilities allow these discounts to be deducted from the cost of a resource. This subject is discussed in greater detail in Section 5.4.
Links to suppliers	Many CAE systems incorporate sub-systems for obtaining quotations from suppliers and sub-contractors and for analysing the quotations submitted by them. These facilities allow estimators to associate resources with various suppliers. Further details are provided in Section 5.3.
Order quantity factors	Most materials are available in fixed quantities (e.g. bricks are packed in pallets of 500). These factors allow estimators to round up the quantities required for a particular estimate to the nearest orderable quantity.
Awaiting quotes marker	CAE systems allow resource costs to be updated at any stage of the estimating process prior to tender adjudication. This 'marker' allows estimators to identify resources for which quotations have not been received so that suppliers and/or sub-contractors can be chased.
Wastage factors	Allowances for wastage may be added either to resources or items. When included at resource level, they are usually for breakages that occur whilst materials are in transit between suppliers and a construction site. Wastage at item level is described in Table 3.2.
Bulking factors/ conversions	Where aggregates are purchased per cubic metre, bulking factors enable estimators to allow for changes in volume that occur as a result of varying moisture content of the aggregates. (Whilst these facilities may be used infrequently for UK estimates, more regular use is likely in drier climates.)
Heading type	Print-outs of resources may be enhanced by headings, sub-headings and so on. One way of achieiving this is to 'flag' resource descriptions as headings, and this is the purpose of the 'heading type'. Such resource descriptions are then printed out in a different way to other resources.
Currency conversion factors	Many large construction companies frequently submit tenders priced in a foreign currency. Where quotations for labour, plant, materials and sub-contract resources are obtained from overseas sources, these and other facilities allow for conversion to local currency.
Indexes for inflation	Some CAE systems provide facilities which allow estimators to anticipate the escalated cost of resources by a predicted inflation index. These are used with fixed price contracts.
Cost codes	These are used to summarise the costs of resources into categories corresponding to a company's cost monitoring system.
Sort codes	Resource reports are generally arranged in a sequence dictated by resource codes (or by cost codes where these are used). This may not be appropriate in certain circumstances and 'sort codes' may be used to structure data in a different way.

Table 3.1 (*continued*)

Facility	Explanation
Weighting factors	These may be used to alter library data to reflect the conditions on a particular estimate. For example, if estimators consider that labour in a certain area is ten per cent more efficient than the data stored in their library, the global entry of a suitable weighting factor will make this alteration for that estimate.
Mark-ups	These factors generally allow estimators to add percentages or amounts to the cost of a resource or a category of resources. This aspect is dealt with in Section 6.3.2.
Comments	Some systems allow for the entry of text to record notes such as details of problems experienced with a certain material, alternative materials and so on.

CAE systems frequently allow these categories to be chosen by estimators and in many cases other categories (such as transport and scaffolding) may also be included. The data stored for resources varies from system to system but certain aspects are considered as prerequisites. These include:

- a **code** identifying each resource (e.g. L01)
- a **description** (e.g. Labourer)
- the **units of measurement** that the resource is supplied in (e.g. hours)
- the **cost per unit** (e.g. £5.50 per hour)

Many CAE systems allow several additional factors to be stored for each resource. The list shown in Table 3.1 is indicative of those that estimators wish to consider and that are provided by various CAE systems. (Note that, for convenience, factors which relate to both **estimating libraries** and to **estimates** are provided in Table 3.1.)

It is sometimes convenient not to enter data in certain fields. For example, quotations are generally obtained for all materials and sub-contract items with significant cost implications for every estimate prepared. This makes any cost data stored in an estimating library of historical interest only. Some estimators thus leave the **cost per unit** field blank in their library and only enter up-to-date costs for estimates. Blank resource costs warn that quotations are still required as, during the preparation of an estimate, resources reports highlight this unpriced data. **Currency conversion** and **mark-up** factors (see Table 3.1) are also generally left blank in libraries as they are dependent on the requirements of individual estimates.

Although resources are generally used to incorporate **money** into estimating calculations, this is not their only function. CAE systems also calculate the total **quantity** of each resource used in a bill of quantities. This is particularly useful not only to estimators but also to buyers, planners and those involved in adjudicating estimates. Some of the different ways in which each of these parties uses this information are described below.

- Summaries of resource quantities may be used by **estimators** to assist in obtaining an overall perception of the work involved in certain elements of construction. For example, a comparison of the resource total of bricklayer hours to that of bricks will help estimators to take a view of the production rates they use for brickwork.
- **Buyers** need to inform suppliers of the total quantities of resources that are to be purchased so that quantity related discounts may be negotiated.
- **Planners** use this information to reconcile the resource requirements they calculate for their tender construction programmes to the resource quantities calculated by estimators.
- **Adjudication panels** use these quantities to gain an appreciation of the size and scope of an estimate. When 'fixed price' tenders are called for, these data are also useful in helping management quantify the risks associated with categories of resource costs escalating at different rates to other categories.

CAE systems produce resource quantities for all the resources contained within items. However, estimators may require certain resource quantities that are not readily calculated unless items are structured in a particular way. Consider the total quantity of concrete used in an estimate. This 'bulk' quantity is frequently used by estimators, planners and management to help provide an appreciation of the size and complexity of a project. To calculate this, all the item quantities for the various different strengths of concrete found in a bill of quantities need to be added together. However, the way in which CAE systems calculate these quantities is based on the resources contained within each item and not on the item quantities themselves. If items are built up in the normal way, CAE systems will only calculate the total quantities for each strength of concrete. This may be overcome by using 'dummy' resources (i.e. resources which are not priced and which do not influence the cost of bill items) in all concrete items. CAE systems are then able to calculate the total quantity of concrete based on all concrete mixes regardless of strength. This approach may be extended to include the amounts contributed by sundry concrete items (such as those described per square metre, per linear metre and so on). It may obviously be applied to other building elements, e.g. brickwork, formwork, plastering and so on.

Bulk quantities are also used in the calculation of average rates. Average rates are calculated by dividing the total cost of a particular element (e.g. brickwork) by the total quantity of that element (e.g. the overall area, or 'bulk quantity', of brickwork). (Elemental costs may be calculated by the judicious use of the item sort codes described in Table 3.2.) Average rates calculated from several estimates are, in many cases, referred to by management at adjudication meetings (see also Section 6.2.5).

3.5.2   Gangs

Manual estimating procedures frequently involve calculating 'gang' rates such as the brickwork gang referred to in Figure 3.1. Although this gang is composed entirely of labour resources, other gangs may include labour, materials, plant and sub-contract resources. For example, a mortar gang may include appropriate quantities of cement and sand, as well as a mortar mixer and labour to fill and operate the mixer (as shown in

MORTAR			
Cement	4.5 pkt @ £5.00 per pkt	=	£22.50
Sand	1.25m^3 @ £10.00 per m^3	=	£12.50
			£35.00
	Add 5% wastage	=	£1.75
	Total material cost per m^3	=	£36.75
Mortar mixer			
	1 hr/m^3 @ £10 per hour	=	£10.00
	Total plant cost per m^3	=	£10.00
Labourer			
	1 hr/m^3 @ £4 per hour	=	£4.00
	Total labour cost per m^3	=	£4.00
	Total cost per m^3	=	**£50.75**

Figure 3.5   Example of gang rate

Figure 3.5). Most CAE systems provide facilities which allow resources to be collected together into gangs in this way.

CAE 'gang' facilities generally resemble manual estimating procedures. However, there are major differences in the ways CAE systems provide these facilities. Those which duplicate manual methods are generally more popular than those which use non-traditional ones. Some systems allow gangs to be created as resources and others as items. It is worth noting the relative merits of these approaches as the method chosen impacts on other uses to which CAE systems may be put. An illustration of these methods is given in Figure 3.6 and Figure 3.7.

The **gangs as resources** approach shown in Figure 3.6 is logical to most estimators. Once gangs have been built up they are used within items in a similar way to resources (a procedure which mirrors manual estimating methods). Figure 3.7 shows an alternative approach where gangs are created as **items**. The facilities which CAE systems provide to achieve this are generally similar to those where gangs are collected as resources. However, assembling gangs as items provides greater flexibility in the way other items may be built up. Instances where this arrangement is particularly useful include:

- Elemental build-ups (see Section 3.7). These are collections of items which relate to elements of buildings (e.g. an external wall which consists of an external skin of face brickwork, some cavity wall ties, insulation, internal blockwork, plasterboard and so on). Where a CAE system uses the 'gangs as items' approach shown in Figure 3.7, elemental facilities are generally easier and more logical to use.
- Bill items which are priced in an identical manner to other items. Many bills of quantities provide identical bill descriptions in various sections of a bill (e.g. brickwork items in **Substructure**, **Superstructure** and **External Works** sections). In these cases, it is convenient for estimators to be able to call up the original build-

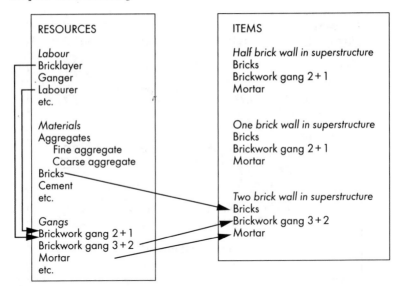

Figure 3.6   Gangs assembled as resources

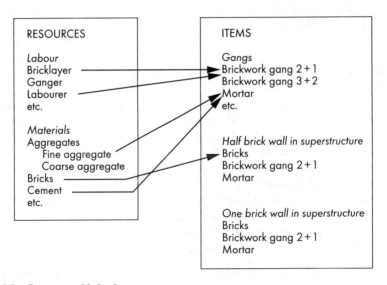

Figure 3.7   Gangs assembled as items

up of an item and refer to it (perhaps with additions and/or alterations) on subsequent occasions. The 'gangs as items' approach is ideally suited to this requirement.

Most CAE systems allow gangs to contain other gangs. So, for example, the labourer rate shown in Figure 3.5 might be structured as a gang comprising all the elements of an

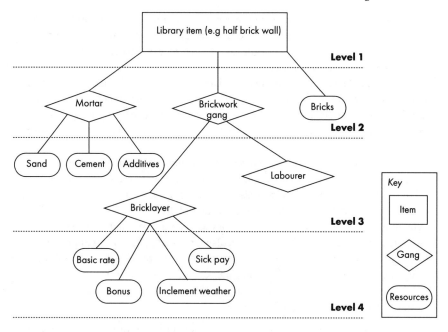

Figure 3.8 Nesting of gangs within gangs

all-in labour rate (such as basic rate, guaranteed minimum bonus, inclement weather, sick pay, and so on). Many systems allow this structure of gangs within gangs to occur for several levels. This is illustrated in Figure 3.8 where a brickwork item is shown to contain a mortar gang, a brickwork gang and a resource of bricks. The brickwork gang in turn is comprised of a bricklayer gang and a labourer gang, with their resources being contained at level 4. The depth of levels that may be provided within an item is of key importance when CAE systems are used for elemental estimating (see Section 3.7). In practice estimators seldom build up items (or elements) that are more than six to eight levels deep (though many CAE systems allow for more than this).

The advantages of gang rates are as follows:

- Using gang build-ups means that there is less **repetition of data** in a library or estimate. Gangs (such as mortar shown in Figure 3.5) are assembled once and used many times. Without gang facilities, resources need to be entered for every occasion they were required. This is a tedious and repetitive process.
- Gangs need to be revised from time to time and CAE facilities provide additional benefits over manual methods in this regard. The first relates to updating costs. As already mentioned in Section 3.3, the **resource based** approach which most CAE systems use ensures that item rates are automatically recalculated according to any changes in resource costs that are made. Gangs, like items, are automatically revised when resource data are changed. These changes, in turn, automatically impact on other items containing gangs (i.e. the hierarchical structure of items which contain

gangs – which may in turn contain other gangs – does not restrict this updating process). So, for example, altering the cost of cement will cause the rates of mortar gangs, concrete gangs and plaster gangs as well as brickwork items, concrete items and plastering items to be revised.

The second benefit of gang build-ups relates to changes in gang data (rather than in the cost of constituent resources). Where output rates, wastage factors and so on are changed, the effort necessary to update gang costs using manual methods is considerable. Using a CAE system significantly reduces the effort required to revise gangs.

The third benefit of CAE gang rates over manually calculated ones becomes apparent as the estimating process progresses. CAE systems accumulate quantities of all the resources used in gangs in the same way as resource quantities are collected for bill items. This makes it possible to obtain details of, for example, the quantity of cement used in mortar, the amount of labour used to service a mortar mixer, and so on. Although these quantities may be calculated manually, the effort required is prohibitive. CAE systems generally do not automatically provide quantities of the gang rates used in an estimate (i.e. cubic metres of mortar used and so on). Where estimators require this information, 'dummy resources' (as described in Section 3.5.1) need to be incorporated in gang build-ups.

Gang rates provide powerful tools which mimic manual procedures and enhance the ease with which items may be assembled. The judicious use of gangs is a distinguishing feature of the effective use and understanding of CAE systems.

3.6 UNIT RATE ESTIMATING

As already mentioned, unit rate estimating is the most popular method of calculating rates for building estimates. The methods which CAE systems use to achieve this vary considerably but certain data are common to all systems. These are:

- A **code** identifying each item (e.g. HBWB).
- A **description** (e.g. 110 mm brick superstructure wall in Class B mortar).
- The **units of measurement** that the item is described in (e.g. square metres).
- The **resources** and/or **gangs** of which the item is comprised (e.g. bricks, brickwork gang and mortar).
- The **production rates** for each of these resources and/or gangs. A **production** rate may be defined as how long it takes to produce something (e.g. one-and-a-half minutes per brick) whereas an **output** rate refers to how much is produced per unit of time (e.g. a bricklayer laying bricks at a rate of 40 per hour). The term **usage** is also sometimes used where the quantity of materials per unit is to be entered (e.g. 60 bricks are required per square metre of half brick wall). For clarity the term 'production rate' is used in this book to refer to production, output and usage rates.

The manner in which CAE systems cater for these rates differs significantly between CAE systems. Two main methods predominate:

Table 3.2 Facilities provided with items

Facility	Explanation
Wastage factors	As already mentioned (in Table 3.1), waste may be taken into account at either resource or item level. When added to items, some CAE systems allow wastage factors to be applied to individual components (i.e. a resource or a gang), as well as to all components (i.e. the item itself).
Number of uses	Most formwork items require the use of a division factor so that the cost of materials may be divided by the number of times it will be re-used. This facility allows this to occur.
Heading types	Print-outs of items may be enhanced by using headings, sub-headings and so on. Most CAE systems provide options which identify item descriptions as headings and then print them out in a way that distinguishes them from other items.

Escalation codes	These facilities may be required in two instances:
	– Estimators need to predict increased costs on 'Fixed Price' tenders. Escalation codes may be used to sort and total bill items to show the financial commitment of construction work classified under each escalation index.
	– If the data provided by CAE systems are to be used by 'Valuations' packages to prepare interim claims for construction work
	    and
	if construction contractors are to be compensated for increased costs due to inflation (by the application of escalation indices such as the Baxter indices)
	    then
	each item needs to be related to a relevant escalation index.

Sort codes	Estimators frequently want to consider bill items in a different order from that determined by bill page/item references. Sort codes allow for alternative sequences to be provided. Typically, sort codes may include the geographic areas of a building, work sections (or trades) and so on.
Difficulty factors	Many estimators consider the data stored in libraries to represent their company's norms of production. When preparing an estimate, it may be convenient to apply a factor to all production/output rates corresponding to the anticipated ease (or difficulty) of constructing a particular project. This may be because, for example, the productivity of labour expected in a certain geographical area is above (or below) the norm. Difficulty factors allow library data to remain unaltered whilst production rates for specific estimates are changed.
Activity link	A few CAE systems allow bill items to be linked to activities in planning systems and 'activity links' facilitate this. However, few software vendors provide both CAE and planning systems and in these circumstances, creating such links can be cumbersome.
Mark-up	These factors generally allow estimators to add percentages or amounts to the cost of items or a category of items. This aspect is dealt with in Section 6.3.2.
Comments	Some systems allow for text to be entered to record, for example, why particular production rates were used and so on. This information is particularly useful in communicating estimators' ideas to site management for those tenders that are won.

- Some systems require these rates to be entered in a specific format (i.e. they provide specific fields for production rates to be inserted). With this approach additional fields are also provided to cater for the other factors described in Table 3.2.
- Other systems provide facilities which allow estimators to develop their own formulae to reflect the production rate in question. Here estimators use recognised symbols to invoke arithmetical functions (e.g. + (plus), − (minus), / (divide), * (multiply) and so on). In some cases, user-defined constants may also be incorporated in a formula.

There are advantages and disadvantages to these approaches. Being able to develop formulae appeals to many estimators as it allows them the flexibility to calculate rates in their own way. In addition, some estimators feel constrained by having to insert production rates in a specific way. However, there is a cost to this flexibility. Where **wastage factors, number of uses, difficulty factors** and so on are provided as separate fields by a CAE system (see Table 3.2), **resource quantities** and **monetary amounts** relevant to each of these factors may be calculated. Estimators are thus able to see, for example, the total quantity of 'waste' bricks and their associated cost (which may be calculated either for a complete bill, sections of a bill or for individual items). This information is particularly useful at the time when an estimate is adjudicated. It is, however, not provided by systems which allow estimators to develop their own formulae.

Many CAE systems provide several additional facilities which may be incorporated in item calculations. The list shown in Table 3.2 is indicative of those that estimators may wish to consider. (Note that, for convenience, factors which relate to both **estimating libraries** and to **estimates** are provided here.)

3.7   ELEMENTAL BUILD-UPS

Elemental build-ups are created by combining several items in specific proportions. For example, an elemental build-up for a ground floor slab might include appropriate quantities of hardcore, damp proof membrane, insulation, concrete, screed and so on. They are ideally suited to situations where estimators have the latitude to prepare estimates that are *not* based on bills of quantities. Such situations include 'design and build' projects and repetitive construction such as housing.

The need for discipline in structuring estimating data is emphasised throughout this book and it is especially pertinent where libraries are developed for elemental estimating. If item libraries are effectively structured, they may provide data for estimates based on bills of quantities as well as for those measured elementally. Figure 3.9 illustrates this point by categorising item data into three layers.

- *Layer 1* The data held here are resources and gangs (see Sections 3.5.1 and 3.5.2) which are used as building blocks of layer 2 items. It is worth repeating that some estimators only use CAE systems to update the costs of gang rates (such as brickwork gangs, concrete, mortar gangs and so on) and do not progress further than this layer in collecting library data. In such cases gangs are used to assist in calculating the costs of bill items from first principles and no further use is made of library facilities. See Section 5.2.2 for further details of this approach.

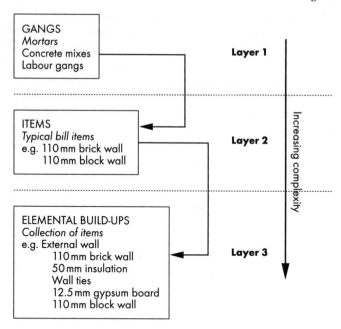

Figure 3.9 Elemental estimating

- *Layer 2* Layer 2 items are used to prepare estimates for bills of quantities. Suitable library item build-ups are linked to items found in bills of quantities as described in Section 5.2.
- *Layer 3* The elemental build-ups created in layer 3 are collections of layer 2 items in appropriate proportions.

Layer 2 items may be those normally used for bills of quantities estimating or they may have been created specifically for elemental build-ups. It is in the first instance that the benefits of a well thought out data structure become apparent. Where data have been arranged to service the requirements of both bills of quantities *and* elemental estimating, the same library may be used for these purposes (i.e. estimates based on bills of quantities draw on layer 2 items and elemental estimates access layer 3 items). This arrangement has the advantage of ensuring a consistent approach to estimating within an organisation and, in addition, simplifies the updating of library data.

An area where the benefits of using computer systems for elemental estimating have been recognised is in the housing industry. One of the main advantages of this approach is that it **rationalises the measurement process**. The following examples illustrate this:

- *External wall elements* It is possible to create elements for a linear metre of foundation wall which contain all the labour, plant and materials involved in its construction. Some CAE systems provide facilities which allow users to enter a variable within an element which allows the height of such foundation walls to be changed according to the depth of excavation required.

■ *Window (or door) elements*   Elements which contain the resources and gangs for building a window or door into a wall may also be assembled (e.g. frame, cavity closers, lintels, sills, paint and so on). However, the quantities of external wall resources need to be reduced as a result of the openings created by the windows/ doors. Elemental build-ups containing negative areas (corresponding to that of the window or door being built in) of external wall elements may be built up. These automatically make all the time consuming adjustments normally associated with openings.

The repetitive nature of this type of construction makes the effort required to develop data in this way worthwhile. It is also worth noting that some success has been experienced in the housing industry linking dimensions generated by CAD systems to elemental build-ups. Lengths of walls, floor areas, numbers of doors and so on are generated by a CAD system and passed to a CAE system providing almost instant feedback on the cost implications of designs.

As estimators have become more and more familiar with CAE systems, they have looked for ways in which to use them more effectively. Elemental estimating provides one such method and has attracted increasing attention in recent times.

3.8   OPERATIONAL RATE ESTIMATING

The **resource based** approach is ideally suited to **unit rate** estimating, but may also be applied to **operational** estimating. This approach, although used most commonly in civil engineering estimates, may also be used for building projects. McCaffer and Baldwin (1991) define it as: '. . . the calculation of a direct cost rate for labour and plant based upon the total quantity of work involved and the total period that resources will be required on site. . .'.

The placing of concrete in the sub-structure of a building, for example, usually includes many different bill items (concrete in bases, ground beams, ground bearing slabs and so on). Where estimators wish to consider the labour and plant requirements of these items within the same period, operational calculations ensure that unproductive time is accounted for in item rate calculations. Not all CAE systems provide operational rate facilities and where they are available, the mechanism by which they work varies from system to system.

3.9   EXTENDING THE RESOURCE BASED APPROACH

An extension to the resource based approach described in Section 3.3 of this chapter has recently been developed. It recognises the problems associated with collecting a large amount of estimating data in a library and has as its aim the simplification of this task. It provides facilities which allow estimators to develop computer models of the various ways in which items are to be built up. This is best explained by comparing it with the traditional resource based approach. When, for example, a brickwork library is

04 Brickwork	01 Foundations 05 Superstructure	01 Brick on edge 05 110mm thick	A Class A mortar B Class B mortar

Figure 3.10 Classification of brickwork items

developed, items are stored for combinations of codes presented in a brickwork classification similar to that shown in Figure 3.10. In this example estimators need to store data for code 040101A (Brick on edge wall in foundations in Class A mortar), 040101B (Brick on edge wall in foundations in Class B mortar) and so on. If items for all possible combinations of codes are held in a library, this approach becomes unworkable. Not only is an appreciable amount of disk storage space required, but certain combinations of codes never occur in practice. In Figure 3.10, for example, there are unlikely to be many bills of quantities that call for 'brick-on-edge' walls in foundations, and storing infrequently used data in a library serves little purpose (see also Chapter 4).

The new approach recognises the inefficiencies described above and provides facilities which allow estimators to develop item build-ups which recognise and act on selections made by estimators. With this method estimators select combinations of codes from a classification similar to Figure 3.10. Having done this, the CAE system selects appropriate data according to rules previously defined by estimators.

3.10 SUMMARY

Virtually all CAE systems used by contractors' estimators adopt the resource based approach to estimating. Varying amounts of data are stored in their estimating libraries and this is achieved in different ways. The data stored comprises resources, gangs and items. In some cases operational build-ups are also held but this approach has so far not gained popularity with most building estimators. In contrast, elemental build-ups are being used increasingly, especially by house builders.

3.11 REFERENCES

Cole G (1995). Bob's your answer. Windows 95 Supplement to *The Times*, 24 August.
Harrison R (1995). Consultation with R Harrison (FCIOB), Managing Director, Manifest Systems Ltd, September 1995.
McCaffer R and Baldwin A N (1991). *Estimating and tendering for civil engineering works*, second edition. BSP Professional, ISBN 0632029528.
McCaffer R and Sher W (1981). Computer aided estimating – an interactive approach. *Building Technology and Management*, Vol. 19, No. 2, February. ISSN 0009-3709.

CHAPTER 4

METHODS OF CLASSIFYING AND CODING LIBRARY DATA

4.1 SCOPE

This chapter describes the requirements of classification and coding systems for storing data in an estimating library. Some of the problems that may be experienced in storing these data are outlined as well as ways in which these may be overcome.

4.2 INTRODUCTION

As described in Chapter 3, CAE systems provide various ways for estimators to store resources and items in an estimating library. Being able to find these data when they are required is key to how effective these systems are in use. Equally important is being able to store new data in a suitable location so that they may easily be identified and retrieved at a later date. This cannot be achieved unless estimators plan how data are to be organised. There are two prerequisites for this, i.e. a classification and a coding system. For the sake of clarity, a **classification** is defined as an arrangement of similar subjects and a **coding system** as a set of symbols used to identify the subjects in the classification. As already mentioned in the previous chapter, CAE systems require each resource and item to be identified by a code. A well thought out classification and associated coding system will allow:

- existing data to be found when required
- new data to be stored in a suitable location
- new data to be found when required.

Poorly constructed systems provide none of these and are cumbersome to use.

4.3 WHAT MAKES A GOOD CLASSIFICATION AND CODING SYSTEM?

What factors influence the quality of a classification and a coding system? Many CAE systems may be purchased complete with estimating libraries and thus provide their own classifications and coding systems. If estimators are to assess the efficacy of these systems (or if they find them unsuitable and wish to develop their own), a general set of principles is useful. This chapter provides such guidance. Although classifications and coding systems are intrinsically linked together, it is convenient to consider them separately.

4.3.1 Classification systems

Three different classifications for the same set of Groundwork data are illustrated in Figures 4.1 to 4.3.

Figure 4.1 is likely to confuse everyone. It simply lists the various bill items catered for. It is extremely difficult to interpret and anyone trying to establish the code of, for example, 'Excavating top soil to be preserved, average depth 300 mm' would be hard pressed to arrive at 'D.2.1.1'.

In Figure 4.2 the judicious and consistent use of spaces makes all the difference. It is easier to understand and codes for individual items can be derived relatively easily.

Figure 4.3 provides a different form of presentation. It emphasises the distinction between the various parts of the bill item descriptions in a hierarchical manner. This arrangement also assists estimators in arriving at codes for specific items. Furthermore, it is economical in terms of space, i.e. it is possible to present more data on a printed page than with the previous examples. This means that those using these classifications do not have to page through as much information to locate a specific item code.

What is to be learnt from these examples? It is obvious that the manner in which a classification is presented is important, but what else has an influence? Stewart (1979) identified several factors which contribute to good design whilst investigating the

```
D EXCAVATION AND EARTHWORKS
.1 SITE PREPARATION
.1 Excavating top soil to be preserved, average depth
.1 150 mm
.2 300 mm
.2 EXCAVATION GENERALLY
.1 Excavating starting at natural ground level or reduced ground level
.1 Excavating to reduce levels, maximum depth not exceeding
.1 0.25 m
.2 1.00 m
.3 2.00 m
.4 4.00 m
.2 Excavating for basements, maximum depth not exceeding
.1 0.25 m
.2 1.00 m
.3 2.00 m
.4 4.00 m
```

Figure 4.1 Classification of Groundwork items

```
D EXCAVATION AND EARTHWORKS
   .1 SITE PREPARATION
        .1 Excavating top soil to be preserved, average depth
             .1 150 mm
             .2 300 mm
   .2 EXCAVATION GENERALLY
        .1 Excavating starting at natural ground level or reduced ground level
             .1 Excavating to reduce levels, maximum depth not exceeding
                  .1 0.25 m
                  .2 1.00 m
                  .3 2.00 m
                  .4 4.00 m
        .2 Excavating for basements, maximum depth not exceeding
             .1 0.25 m
             .2 1.00 m
             .3 2.00 m
             .4 4.00 m
```

Figure 4.2   Indented classification of excavation and earthworks items

D EXCAVATION AND EARTHWORKS	1 SITE PREPARATION	1 Excavating top top soil to be preserved, average depth	1 150 mm 2 300 mm	
	2 EXCAVATION GENERALLY	1 Excavating starting at natural or reduced ground level	1 Excavating to reduce levels maximum depth not exceeding	1 0.25 m 2 1.00 m 3 2.00 m 4 4.00 m
			2 Excavating for basements, maximum depth not exceeding	1 0.25 m 2 1.00 m 3 2.00 m 4 4.00 m

Figure 4.3   Hierarchical classification of Groundwork items

manner in which information is displayed on computer screens. These factors are equally relevant to the design of classifications and include:

- *Logical sequence*   The sequence in which information is presented should be logical and should, wherever possible, follow accepted practice. For example, a system for classifying building data which arranged bill items in an order different from SMM7 (1988) would not be accepted by most building estimators.
- *Spaciousness*   Spacing and blanks are important to emphasise and maintain a logical sequence or structure. This is readily apparent when Figures 4.1 and 4.2 are compared. All that is different between them is that text in Figure 4.2 has been

indented to indicate a logical structure. Spacing and blanks also help to identify and recognise items of information – a cluttered classification greatly increases the time necessary to search for items of information and also increases the likelihood of missing or overlooking items and misreading items.

- *Relevance*   It is usual for developers of classifications to try and provide those using their systems with information of real and potential relevance. In many cases, information of potential relevance only leads to confusion and should therefore be excluded. For example, it is clearly necessary for classifications to distinguish between common, facing and engineering bricks. However, it is questionable whether details of all the different bricks produced by all brick manufacturers should be included.
- *Consistency*   Classifications that are consistently structured and presented allow unfamiliar sections to be more readily and accurately interpreted. In addition, they should conform to existing practices in the use of language and structure. This aspect was also recognised by Gilb (1980) who states that 'rules for the design of codes for any given system should be ... consistently followed'.
- *Grouping*   Where there are relationships between items, presentation can be improved if relevant items are grouped together. This is highlighted in Figure 4.3 by the use of horizontal and vertical lines which emphasise groups of similar data. Grouping may also be assisted by the use of CAPITAL LETTERS, and `different fonts`. The examples above show that a simple technique such as using capital letters further assists in defining groups of similar data or relationships between data. In addition, *italics* and **bold** typefaces may also be used in conjunction with *CAPITALISATION* to provide a set of tools for developers of classifications to use. For those with larger budgets, colour may also be used to emphasise logical groupings.
- *Simplicity*   All the above factors need to be taken into account, but the overriding principle should be to present the **appropriate quantity** and **level** of information in the **simplest way**.

Two other factors apply specifically to classifications of estimating data:

- *Level of detail*   Estimating classifications cannot cater for the multitude of different items that occur in bills of quantities. The sheer volume of potential items makes this impracticable and, as already mentioned, having infrequently used data permanently available causes problems. However, these systems should cater for standard items of work. For example, a contractor specialising in industrial buildings will develop systems relating to that building type, whilst another contractor with a more varied workload will require systems to cope with a more general range of data. The degree to which these systems are developed and refined to cater for more unusual items thus depends upon the requirements of each organisation.
- *Descriptions of materials*   Similarly it is not practicable to include detailed materials descriptions in CAE classifications. Catering for all the numerous different components that may be used in the construction of any bill item serves little purpose as many of these data will be used infrequently. The effort required to collect such data does not justify the benefit they will provide. However, estimators do need to distinguish between different materials as there are obvious cost implications. One

way of developing classification systems that cater for this is to consider whether the choice of material has an implication on the **rate of production** or not. For example, the cost of pouring concrete of strength 'A' or strength 'B' in a given location will not vary noticeably. However, any difference in reinforcement content is likely to have a significant effect on productivity and consequently on the cost of the placed concrete. Materials should be allocated in an ad hoc manner into broad categories (e.g. heavily reinforced concrete, lightly reinforced concrete, mass concrete and so on) and incorporated into classifications on this basis.

Table 4.1   Code 324

Classification	In this case none has been adopted. The item in question is simply the 324th consecutive entry in an item library.
Advantages	The code is short.
Disadvantages	Problems are immediately experienced when a reasonably substantial amount of data has been collected. The main ones are: – that of locating existing items (as expected, when a specific item of data is required, it can be tedious to find), and – storing new data in its logical position (this is not possible!).

Table 4.2   Code 1012

Classification	A very basic system has been used to generate this code. Of the 9999 items available in this item classification, the range of numbers from 1000 to 1999 has been reserved for brickwork. Within this range, the first 20 have been reserved for walls 110 mm thick and this particular item is the twelfth entry. No further classification has been attempted.
Advantages	The code is short.
Disadvantages	– Some limited expansion has been allowed for. – It is difficult to decipher the code without reference to a classification (or *code book* as some estimators call it).

Table 4.3   Code 4222

Classification	In this example a four tier hierarchical classification has been adopted. The first level (in this case 4) relates to the building trade, and subsequent levels define additional detail.

4 Brickwork	1 Foundations	1 Brick on edge	1 Class A mortar
	2 Superstructure	2 110 mm thick	2 Class B mortar

Advantages	– The code is still short. – Familiarity with the system allows users to recognise bill items from their codes (e.g. all superstructure brickwork items begin with 42, and so on).
Disadvantages	It allows limited opportunities for expansion (i.e. ten entries within any level). If more than this number is required, items will be stored out of sequence.

Table 4.4   Code 040505B

Classification	The classification used here is a development of that shown in Table 4.3. The key differences are:
	– Extra characters have been allocated to allow additional items to be entered at some later date.
	– Alpha characters have also been used to make the code more recognisable (e.g. B for Class B mortar). It is worth noting that alpha characters provide more opportunity for expansion than numbers (i.e. one alpha character represents 26 options compared to ten when a number is used).

04 Brickwork	01 Foundations	01 Brick on edge	A Class A mortar
	05 Superstructure	05 110 mm thick	B Class B mortar

Advantages	The code allows more opportunity for future expansion. Two digits have been reserved in each of the first three levels and an alpha field has been provided in the fourth.
Disadvantages	The code is longer than any of the previous examples.

Table 4.5   Code HBWB

Classification	No formal classification has been used.
Advantages	– The code is easily recognisable (and resembles abbreviations in common use in the construction industry).
	– The code is short.
Disadvantages	Logical arrangement of data is not possible.

4.3.2   Coding systems

The main requirement of a coding system identified so far is that it should facilitate further data being added to an estimating library without the logical structure of existing data being compromised. There are several more requirements and the examples provided in Tables 4.1 to 4.5 highlight them.

Consider some codes for a typical brickwork item – 110 mm brick superstructure wall in Class B mortar.

Before considering the next example, it is worth illustrating the manner in which most computer systems store data. In the case of a three character numeric code (e.g. 45, 144, 9, etc.), data are arranged from the lowest number to the highest based, firstly, on the left-most digit, then the second from left, and so on. Thus, for the codes 45, 144, 9, computer systems will store 144 first, followed by 45 and then 9. If these numbers are to be stored in ascending order, leading zeros need to be inserted (i.e. 009, 045, 144). This has implications on the number of characters that need to be provided at each level (and consequently the length of codes) as illustrated in Table 4.4.

These examples highlight some of the aspects to be considered when designing a CAE coding system. They are:

- *Unique identification*   Most authorities (including Gilb [1980], Crisp [1966], and Gilchrist and Gaster [1969]) agree that this is the most important requirement of a coding system. Each item of estimating data needs to be able to be identified by a unique and unambiguous reference.
- *Length of code*   Codes should be as short as possible. There are several factors which support this requirement, namely:
    (a) *Resistance to long codes*   Practising estimators dislike long codes – this has been documented by Moyles (1973) and Bradburn (1974). This was also found to be the case in the allied field of quantity surveying where Scoins (1980) noted that many practising quantity surveyors had experienced the 'nightmare' of lengthy codes when using computer systems to assist in preparing bills of quantities.
    (b) *Errors in identifying correct code*   There is always a chance of making a mistake when trying to find the code corresponding to an item of data. Where codes are long this situation is exacerbated as there is even more opportunity for mistakes to be made.
    (c) *Errors in entering a code into a computer system*   Similarly, errors may occur when entering codes into a computer system. A long code is likely to increase the chance of this happening.
    (d) *Time taken to enter a code*   The longer a code is, the more time it will take to enter into a computer system. Bills of quantities frequently contain hundreds of items, each of which may be linked to several codes. Obviously the shorter the code is, the quicker it will be to enter into a CAE system. As one of the potential benefits of using a CAE system is that it assists in producing estimates more quickly than manual methods, this is of key importance. The implications of including unnecessary characters may be appreciated by comparing the codes resulting from the classifications shown in Figures 4.1 and 4.3. The decimal point used to delimit fields in Figure 4.1 serves no purpose and results in a code (D.2.1.1) requiring seven keystrokes, whereas the same item in Figure 4.3 requires four (D211).
    (e) *Time taken to find a code*   Keeping a code as short as possible may lengthen the time needed to find a specific item of data. This is best illustrated by considering the extremes of short and long codes. When short codes are used, the resulting classifications are likely to be lengthy (and, when printed out, will probably extend over several pages). The classifications on which Tables 4.1 and 4.2 have been based would illustrate these long lists. However, when longer codes are used, classifications tend to spread horizontally and result in a more concise presentation (as illustrated in Tables 4.3 and 4.4). These lists occupy fewer pages than those where short codes are used. In summary, short codes result in long lists to search through and the initial inconvenience of using a longer code may eventually be outweighed.

    In summary, Gilb (1980) states that 'techniques for psychologically shortening long (codes) . . . should be capitalised upon wherever possible'.

In another study by Ruch (1984), it was found that our 'short term memory' is limited to remembering codes of between five and nine digits. This was developed into the 7 ± 2 rule which recommends that codes be limited in length to between five and nine digits. It also emphasises the importance of **spaciousness** and **grouping** already identified for classifications above.

The case for a short code thus appears to be well supported. However, recent developments in the way estimators communicate with CAE systems bring this assertion into question. Section 5.2.1 describes facilities provided by some CAE systems which avoid estimators having to enter codes (referred to as the 'no codes' approach. Section 5.2.1 also explores where the 'no codes' approach may most beneficially be used as there are situations it is not suited to.) In addition, the increased power of the current generation of computers has meant that extremely long codes may be used to identify data (some systems use abbreviated resource and item descriptions as codes!). The case for short codes is therefore not clear-cut and each situation needs to be assessed on its merits.

- *Recognisability of codes*   Those using a classification should easily be able to identify appropriate codes for items found in bills of quantities and vice versa. Crisp (1966) recognised this in the 1960s when he suggested that it should be possible to 'more or less guarantee to get (the code) right first time ... the feasibility of which one can check at the merest glance'. This aspect is equally relevant to current estimating practice.

- *Level of detail*   As already discussed the data stored in an estimating library need to be limited to those which are used on a regular basis. Coding systems should reflect an appropriate level of detail and, as with classifications, need to be developed for each application.

- *Expandability of code*   Following on from the previous point, coding systems should allow for further data to be added at a later date as well as for the addition of extra classification categories. This hallmark of a good system is unfortunately usually only apparent when it is absent! Expandability has been recognised by Gilb (1980) and Crisp (1966): Crisp (1966) highlights the problems associated with adding to classifications when he states that: 'Flexibility of extension within the code structure is essential. The dangers of overspill and its inevitable concomitant, the amendment of established codes, should be guarded against at all costs.'

- *Descriptions of materials*   As already mentioned, it is not practicable to cater for all the detailed materials descriptions that occur in construction work. However, estimates do need to reflect the specific materials required for each project. A method of accommodating this apparent contradiction is given in Section 4.4.

- *Accommodating dimensions*   In order to store performance data relevant to various items, CAE classifications and coding systems need to reflect dimensions. Bill items (for example, projections in brickwork, rebates in concrete and so on) and resources (for example, doors, windows, pieces of timber, reinforcement, etc.) obviously need to be specified in this manner but the implications of providing for this requirement on the length of codes are daunting. A method of accomplishing this is also given below.

- *Option for choice of method*   When calculating the rate for an item, an estimator's choice of resources depends upon many considerations (for example, the quantity of work involved, restrictions on working conditions, the height of the work above ground level and so on). Again, it is clearly impracticable to cater for the multitude of different ways of, for example, placing concrete in a column. However, it may be worthwhile storing data for some of the construction methods commonly used. This may be provided for in a further classification level (and associated code). In the example of placing concrete in a column, additional options might be included to store data relevant to placing concrete by:

(a)   conveyor
(b)   crane
(c)   pump
(d)   hand

It is worth noting that the need to cater for the peculiarities of each estimate is recognised in most CAE systems. Facilities are generally provided which allow estimators to apply factors which modify the outputs/production rates of the resources, thus accommodating the uniqueness of each situation. Whether or not estimators choose to use these facilities or the options provided by additional library items (or a combination of these approaches) is a matter of personal preference.

Clearly there is no simple formula for devising CAE classifications and coding systems. This section has described a set of (in some cases conflicting) principles to be considered. As all contractors are likely to have their own requirements, the applicability and relative importance of these principles needs to be considered for each organisation. Crisp (1966) sums up the situation well when he suggests a 'basically rigid as well as simple structure' as being a prerequisite of these systems.

4.4   SOME PRACTICAL PROBLEMS AND SOLUTIONS

Experience in implementing and using CAE systems provides a practical insight into classifying and coding data for these systems. The aspects described below reflect some of the experiences of practising estimators.

- *Consistency within classifications*   Ideally a classification should arrange data in a consistent manner. This is particularly important to estimators because the ability to anticipate the structure (and code) of estimating data is likely to speed up the whole estimating process. For example, a bill item classification that always presents trade descriptions first, materials descriptions second and dimensional constraints third will be more efficient to use than one which has a haphazard arrangement. Estimators familiar with a consistent layout will come to expect that, for example, data in the third field relates to dimensions and so on. Any deviation from an established norm is likely to prove disruptive.

  However, most bill classifications do not arrange data in a completely consistent way. Probably the most widely used classification for building works, SMM7 (1988), strives to achieve consistency but does not succeed. The random sample of an excavation and a reinforcement item shown in Figure 4.4 illustrates the problems confronting developers of classifications for construction work. The nature of

D20   Excavating and filling

1 Site prep.	1 Removing trees	1 Girth 600 mm – 1.5 m

E30   Reinforcement for in situ concrete

1 Bar	1 Nominal size	1 Straight	1 Horizontal length 12 – 15 m

Figure 4.4   Sample codes from SMM7

building operations is so varied that rigidly adhering to a consistent structure is likely to be confusing as some items do not require, for example, dimensional constraints. Consistency may also result in longer codes as blank fields need to be inserted where no data are relevant.

The requirement for consistency is laudable but in many cases it is impracticable to achieve. Consistency should be striven for but other considerations (such as the desirability of short codes) may need to take precedence.

- *Expandability of codes*   Additions and alterations to codes may be anticipated and provided for by not coding data consecutively. This is illustrated in Figure 4.5. The gaps provided for in the numbering system allow for some future additions without upsetting the structure of the classification and coding systems.
- *Alpha-numeric codes*   One of the main advantages of using alphabetic characters in codes is that each alpha character provides 26 possibilities (as opposed to ten when numbers are used – one alpha character may thus avoid having to use two numbers). Short codes are desirable, and any method of achieving this is worth serious consideration. Using alpha codes obviously provides an opportunity to do this. In

D GROUNDWORK			
20 EXCAVATION AND FILLING	a SITE PREPARATION	01 Removing trees 05 Removing tree stumps	a Girth 600 mm – 1.50 m e Girth 1.50 – 3.00 m i Girth > 3.00mm
		10 Clearing site vegetation 11 Lifting turf for preservation	
	b EXCAVATION	01 Topsoil for preservation	Average depth: a 250mm
		05 To reduce levels 10 Basements	a 0.25 m e 1.00 m i 2.00 m o 4.00 m

Figure 4.5   Classification for groundwork items

addition, this chapter has already highlighted the importance of **recognisability** when developing a coding system. Alpha characters also help to make codes more recognisable (an example is given in Figure 4.6).

An example of how alpha codes may be used is given in Figure 4.5. Here codes are constructed of alternating alpha and numeric characters. The motivation for this is to provide a consistent structure with which estimators may become familiar (i.e. they come to expect numbers and alpha characters to alternate – and can thus easily identify incorrectly entered codes).

As with all coding systems, problems may occur where more alternatives need to be catered for than can be accommodated by the system adopted. In Figure 4.5, if it is felt that provision needs to be made for increments of less than 250 mm in the depth of excavation in reduced level and basement excavation, the choices provided by a single alpha field will soon be exhausted. It may then be necessary to use a two character alpha field (e.g. aa, ab, ac, etc.). This in turn means that all codes in the fifth field should contain two alpha characters. As this situation frequently occurs when classifications and coding systems have been in use for some time, it is inevitable that some existing codes will not conform to this revised structure.

- *Recognisability of codes*   As already described above, the recognisability of resource and item codes can be improved by using alphabetic characters and numbers. Many abbreviations and shorthand phrases are accepted in the construction industry (for example, n.e. (not exceeding), Ø (diameter) and so on) and may be used as part of codes. In Figure 4.6, BAR and 20 provide visual clues which lead to an intuitive interpretation of the code. Codes which can be deciphered in this way have obvious advantages over those which require reference to a classification. However, codes constructed in this way are likely to be longer than those where a single character is used to represent more data. The advantages of recognisability thus need to be traded off against the costs of lengthening codes.

- *Proliferation of materials*   One way of dealing with the multitude of materials from which buildings may be constructed is to include 'dummy' resources in the estimating library. When items containing these 'dummies' are used in an estimate, the 'dummies' are then changed to match the specific requirements of each estimate (see Figure 1.1). For example, a 'dummy' library resource called 'facing bricks' may be changed to an 'Appleby Medium Grey face brick' for a particular project. Most CAE systems allow this change to be made for the estimate only (i.e. the resources contained in the estimating library are not altered for a tender), and facing bricks may be changed to another type of brick in subsequent estimates.

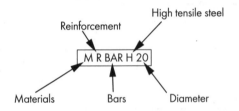

Figure 4.6   Example of a resource code

This approach recognises the fact that current estimating procedure is to obtain a new quotation for all materials for each estimate that is prepared. It provides further motivation to use 'dummy' resources as it is pointless to spend time and effort catering for resources that will, in any case, be re-priced at a later stage.

- *Dimensions in codes*   Where the dimensions of a resource or item need to be included in a code, it is tempting to make these codes recognisable by using the dimension as part of the code (as described for MRBARH20 in Figure 4.6). Accommodating dimensions in this way is not so simple when more than one set of dimensions is involved. For example, a concrete column 200 mm by 200 mm requires seven characters (200 × 200). Codes constructed in this way quickly become excessively long.

Several techniques may be used to reduce this length. Using centimetres instead of millimetres will save two characters – a modest reduction. At the expense of recognisability, two classification fields may be reserved side by side as shown in Figure 4.7.

In this example, 200 mm by 300 mm translates into 'hl', an obvious saving in code length, again at the expense of recognisability.

Another approach is to hold data for a standard (or commonly recurring) component only. These data are then adjusted by multiplying all resource requirements in the item by a factor corresponding to the requirements of a particular project. Most CAE systems provide facilities which will allow this to occur.

4.5   SUMMARY

This chapter first of all identified and described the criteria by which classifications and coding systems may be assessed and developed. Reference was also made to several problems associated with the use of these systems. Solutions to these problems were proposed and it was shown that the effective classification and coding of estimating data needs to be a compromise between the various principles identified.

E20 FORMWORK FOR IN SITU CONCRETE					
13 Beams 14 Beam casings 15 Columns	1 Attached to slabs 2 Attached to walls 3 Isolated	1 Rectangular 2 Square 3 Circular	Width/diameter: a 25 mm b 50 mm c 75 mm d 100 mm e 125 mm f 150 mm g 175 mm h 200 mm i 225 mm j 250 mm k 275 mm l 300 mm	Depth: a 25 mm b 50 mm c 75 mm d 100 mm e 125 mm f 150 mm g 175 mm h 200 mm i 225 mm j 250 mm k 275 mm l 300 mm	Height to soffit: 1 ≤1.50 m 2 1.50 – 3.00 m 3 3.00 – 4.50 m 4 5 6 Left in 7 Permanent

Figure 4.7   Accommodating dimensions within a classification

4.6   REFERENCES

Bradburn S M (1974). The means by which computers can assist estimators. In *Estimating in building and civil engineering*, Northwood Publications.

Crisp P B J (1966). Thoughts on a standard code for the building industry. *The Chartered Surveyor*, March.

Gilb T (1980). Humanised computers: the necessity and payoff. *Computers and People* (USA), May.

Gilchrist A and Gaster K (1969). A study of coding and data co-ordination for the building industry – information systems relating to the construction industry. British Research Station Current Paper 11/69.

Moyles B F (1973). An analysis of the contractor's estimating process. MSc thesis, Loughborough University of Technology.

RICS/BEC (1988). *Standard method of measurement for building works, edition 7* (SMM7), (authorised by agreement between the Royal Institution of Chartered Surveyors and the Building Employers Confederation). Royal Institution of Chartered Surveyors.

Ruch J C (1984). *Psychology, the personal science*. Wadsworth Publishing.

Scoins D (1980). Surveying the computer way. *Building*, 25 July.

Stewart (1979). In B Shackel (ed.) *Man–computer communication: Infotech state of the art report. Vol. 1: Analysis and bibliography*. Infotech.

CHAPTER 5

ESTIMATING PROCEDURE

5.1 SCOPE

This chapter describes the various activities involved in preparing an estimate. It deals with this process from the time a bill of quantities has been entered into a CAE system (as described in Chapter 2) until estimators and/or management are ready to add mark-ups and, by so doing, to convert an estimate into a tender. The first section describes the various ways in which data stored in an estimating library may be linked to the items contained in a bill of quantities. Different ways in which these data may be refined during the estimating period are then described, as well as methods of estimating the costs of 'Preliminary and General' items. An integral part of the estimating process is obtaining quotations from materials suppliers, sub-contractors and plant hire companies, and this is also discussed.

5.2 LINKING BILL ITEMS TO AN ESTIMATING LIBRARY

As described in Chapter 3, estimators may either make extensive use of the estimating data they have accumulated over a period of time in their estimating library, or they may use a more modest amount of data and exploit the calculation facilities offered by CAE systems. The implications on this stage of the estimating process are described below.

5.2.1 'Traditional' computer-aided estimating

Figure 5.1 shows the 'traditional' approach to CAE where data are extracted from an estimating library to assist in estimating the costs of bill items. Figure 5.1 also illustrates that many of these data are refined to meet the particular requirements of an estimate and that inevitably some items need to be built up from first principles. The extent to which data are modified and 'one-off' items built up varies from estimate to estimate and depends also on the extent to which data have been collected.

With this approach, estimators need to link the items found in a bill of quantities with suitable library data. As described in Chapter 4, codes are used to identify data and

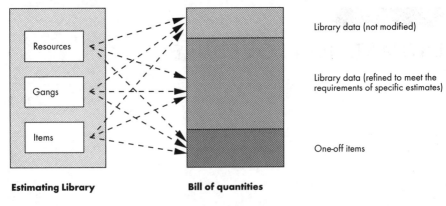

Estimating Library   **Bill of quantities**

Figure 5.1   'Traditional' CAE where library data used in a bill

these are also commonly used to link library data to the bill's items. The main difficulty is how to locate suitable item codes from those stored in an estimating library. There are three different solutions to this problem: the first uses paper-based documents, the second uses the CAE system itself and the third relies on Standard Method of Measurement (SMM) codes provided by clients' quantity surveyors.

- *Paper-based links*   The documents which allow estimators to find suitable data are either print-outs of library data generated by CAE systems (as shown in Figure 5.2), or classifications of these data developed by estimators themselves (as described in Section 4.3.1). Figure 5.2 is based on the same items as those included in the classification shown in Figure 4.7. The advantages and disadvantages of these two documents are set out in Table 5.1.
- *Links within CAE systems*   The problems of finding data (and of devising and maintaining classification and coding systems) have prompted some CAE system vendors to provide computer programs which create and display classification frameworks and coding systems. With this approach, estimators develop their own systems as they accumulate data in their estimating library. These facilities typically divide descriptions into several levels and arrange them in a hierarchical order on a computer screen. In the example shown in Figure 5.3, an estimator looking for

Item code	Item description
040101A	Brickwork in foundations, brick on edge in Class A mortar
040101B	Brickwork in foundations, brick on edge in Class B mortar
040105A	Brickwork in foundations, 110mm thick in Class A mortar
040105B	Brickwork in foundations, 110mm thick in Class B mortar
040501A	Brickwork in superstructure, brick on edge in Class A mortar
040501B	Brickwork in superstructure, brick on edge in Class B mortar
040505A	Brickwork in superstructure, 110mm thick in Class A mortar
040505B	Brickwork in superstructure, 110mm thick in Class B mortar

Figure 5.2   Library item print-out corresponding to classification shown in Table 4.4

Table 5.1   Advantages and disadvantages of print-outs and classifications as a method of locating library data

Library print-outs	Classifications
All the items contained in an estimating library will appear on this print-out.	Only the code of any item may be identified from a classification, i.e. it is difficult to see which codes actually have data stored for them. This is the most serious drawback of this approach as estimators will only find out at a later stage if data for certain items do not exist.
As libraries are revised from time to time, it is inevitable that these print-outs will become obsolete. They thus need to be re-printed from time to time.	Revisions to a classification are simple to effect and do not necessarily require documents to be completely re-printed.
These print-outs are likely to be lengthy documents and will consequently be time consuming to search through.	A classification (such as that shown in Figure 4.7) provides a concise representation of all the items that may be stored in a library. This method thus provides short lists for estimators to search through.

25 mm crushed aggregate first of all selects 'MATERIALS', then 'Aggregates' and so on from successive screens of data until the required resource is found. Provided the progression through these screens is logical (i.e. follows accepted practice, or a pattern that estimators are familiar with) little difficulty is usually experienced in locating data. As estimators decide on this structure themselves, few problems occur in practice.

This approach (referred to as the 'no codes' approach) makes codes appear redundant. Figure 5.3 apparently makes no reference to them as estimators find their way to the data they require by stepping through a series of displays. However, in order to store data in a computer system, a code (or address) *is* required for each item

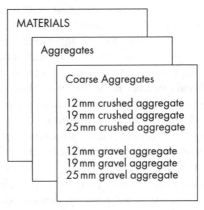

Figure 5.3   Hierarchical structure of resources

of data. The fact that some systems suppress the display of these codes is purely a matter of aesthetics – the codes are still there.

The key difference between systems that adopt this approach and those that do not is that with the 'no codes' method, estimators do not need to refer to other paper documents (such as those compared in Table 5.1) to find codes. They simply sit in front of their computer system and select the data they require. Is this an advantage or a disadvantage? This depends mainly on **who** uses the CAE system and **how frequently** it is used:

(a) *Who uses the system?*   Where estimators operate CAE software themselves, the 'no codes' approach is probably easier to use. However, some estimators prefer to delegate the entry (and sometimes the manipulation) of estimating data to clerical staff (many of whom have been previously employed to 'comp up' manually prepared bills of quantities and are thus familiar with the estimating process). In such circumstances estimators link items in a bill of quantities with suitable data stored in their estimating libraries by writing appropriate codes on the bill. They may also even pencil in adjustments to be made to these data. Clerical staff then enter these codes into their CAE system and, if required, make the necessary adjustments. The 'no codes' approach is clearly not suitable here as clerical staff do not have the expertise (or the authority) to select data from a library. When this is the case, paper-based documents (such as those described above) are required as these estimators are invariably uncomfortable using computer systems.

(b) *How frequently is the system used?*   CAE packages which use the 'no codes' approach are attractive to those not familiar with these systems. (This is especially true at the time of purchase, when software vendors are keen to show to prospective purchasers how 'user-friendly' their software is.) However, once a reasonable level of competence in using a package is reached, having to step through successive screens to access a specific item of data becomes a time consuming way to make a selection. Where CAE packages use the more traditional coded approach, estimators familiar with their estimating library get to know the codes of frequently used data – and are able to call these up extremely quickly. This has obvious advantages over other systems which force users to progress through a series of screen displays.

CAE systems which provide facilities for both approaches are obviously preferable to those which provide one or the other. However, few such systems are currently available. In view of this, the fact that some estimators prefer to operate their systems through clerical staff, and that users' requirements are likely to evolve as their familiarity and competence in using a system increases, coded systems are likely to remain an issue for estimators in the foreseeable future.

- *Standard Method of Measurement codes*   Some bills of quantities include a standard method of measurement code for each bill item (e.g. based on SMM7 [1988] or CESSM3 [1991]). If the coding system provided by the standard method has also been used in an estimator's library an automatic link between each bill item and suitable library data can be made (presuming that appropriate data have already been stored in the library). In practice, this ideal marriage of bill items to library data rarely occurs. The main reason for this is that the coding systems provided by standard methods of measurement allow for individual interpretation of codes. For example, there are numerous occasions where SMM7 (1988) calls for 'specified locations', 'specified handling', 'different cross-section shapes' and so on. As clients' quantity surveyors and contractors' estimators select item codes independently it is highly unlikely that they will arrive at the same code. It is, at least theoretically, possible for such an ideal solution to be developed. However, at the moment the codes used in standard methods of measurement are designed solely to assist in the production of bills of quantities. Obviously this is their main purpose, but there are other uses to which a standard method may be put, and having it serve as a classification and coding system for estimating data is an obvious one. In the United Kingdom, civil and building contractors currently have scant representation on the bodies developing standard methods of measurement and this lack of orientation to estimating is perhaps a result of this.

Once library data have been linked to bill items by one of these methods, it is possible to amend these data according to the particular requirements of each project. This is described in Section 5.5.

5.2.2   CAE systems as calculators

Some estimators question the benefits of storing an extensive estimating library (implied in Figure 5.1) and argue that the effort required to assemble and maintain library data is so great that it makes this approach ineffective. Figure 5.4 shows an alternative approach to estimating where libraries are used primarily to store resources and gangs, the costs of which are revised for each estimate.

Estimators using this approach obviously need to build up rates from first principles for all the items found in a bill of quantities. They justify this approach by comparing it to the procedures that need to be followed when extensive data libraries are used as follows:

- Locating library data that match bill items is time consuming. This is especially true where classifications and coding systems have been poorly devised. In these circumstances the more data stored in a library, the longer it is likely to take to find a specific item (presuming that these data are available in the first place).

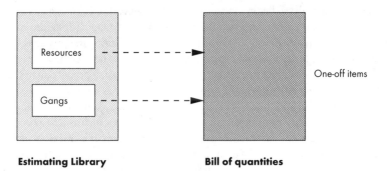

Figure 5.4   Estimating libraries used mainly to facilitate storage and updating of gang rates

- In many cases it is necessary to modify library data according to the specific conditions found on a project. Some estimators feel that they are more productive building up items afresh than making alterations in this way.
- Many UK builders sub-contract much of the work involved in building projects. In these cases library data may be redundant as many of these item rates comprise nothing more than materials quotations and/or sub-contract rates. However, many contractors prepare their own estimates (based on the production rates of their own labour force) to check the costs submitted by sub-contractors. In such circumstances the case for not using library facilities more extensively is unconvincing.

When most of the items in a bill of quantities are built up from first principles, estimators may be tempted to take short-cuts during the preparation of an estimate (e.g. by not entering reasons for their choice of production rates in 'comments' fields, including wastage factors with production rates and so on). This is understandable in the circumstances but detracts from the potential of CAE systems to record all the decisions made during the preparation of an estimate. Indeed, Turner (1995) sees the discipline imposed by CAE systems to 'fully record the logic behind every rate' as an aspect which estimators should welcome as it allows them to obtain feedback on any 'under or over estimates of production rates or materials usage'. Where estimating data is used to prime other computer applications (e.g. interim valuations) this lack of detail is likely to cause confusion and obscure the interpretation of budgets. This aspect is described further in Section 6.4.2.

Whether libraries should be used as comprehensive databases or to store resources and gang rates depends on each construction organisation, the type of work being tendered for and the particular approach favoured by individual estimators. Perhaps the most important part of this whole equation is the commitment of estimators. It is a truism that those involved in selecting a system contribute to its success whilst a cause of failure is frequently lack of participation in the decision making process by these individuals.

5.3   PREPARING REQUESTS FOR QUOTATIONS

With manual methods of estimating it is usual to wait until quotations for resources have been obtained and analysed before starting to calculate item rates. CAE systems are not dependent upon these activities because the resource based structure (described in Section 3.3) allows resource costs to be updated at any stage during the preparation of an estimate. This is not to say that obtaining quotations is a trivial task that may be left to the last moment. Sub-contract items contribute an ever increasing proportion of the overall cost of building estimates in the United Kingdom and as such need to be effectively managed. In addition, all resource costs (i.e. labour, plant, materials and sub-contract) are likely to vary from project to project due to factors such as transport costs, unloading costs, discounts, current market conditions and so on. It is therefore normal current practice to obtain new quotations during the preparation of each estimate. This further emphasises the importance of obtaining and analysing quotations as success in tendering is heavily dependent on it.

The trend to employ sub–contractors has meant that greater emphasis is placed on obtaining quotations for these resources than was the case, say ten years ago. The work that is sub–contracted may involve either a total work package (i.e. a sub–set of a bill of quantities including all the labour and materials required for these items) or the provision of labour-only services (with materials being provided by main contractors). The facilities provided by CAE systems have evolved to meet this important need. A flow chart of the processes involved is provided in Figure 5.5. This shows that bills of quantities data may be processed to collect sub–contract items and quantities of materials, labour and plant. This information may then be assembled together with specifications into an enquiry which is then communicated (usually by post) to suppliers and sub–contractors selected from a supplier/sub–contractor database.

This section focuses on the main information included in the documentation sent out by estimators to sub–contractors and suppliers (hereafter referred to as **requests for quotations**).

5.3.1 Quantities

Quantities are invaluable to the process of obtaining quotations for the following reasons:

- Potential suppliers and sub–contractors need to be informed of the timing and quantity of materials deliveries when quotations are requested (as recommended in the *Code of Estimating Practice* [1983]).
- It is frequently possible to negotiate quantity related discounts with materials suppliers. The task of manually calculating these quantities is time consuming (and may be alleviated by a CAE system as described below).

CAE systems have been developed to assist in providing this information. Two distinct instances occur:

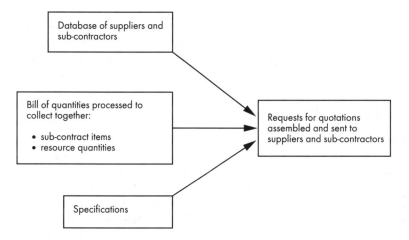

Figure 5.5 Materials and sub–contract enquiry process

- *Quantification of sub-contract work*   To arrive at the total amount of work to be priced by a sub-contractor it is necessary to collect together all bill items relating to the operations of that sub-contractor. These items may be (and often are) distributed widely throughout a bill of quantities (except in the rare instances where bills are produced in an 'elemental' or 'operational' format). Some CAE systems provide 'abstracting' facilities which assist estimators to collect these items together. To achieve this a sort code (as described in Table 3.2) needs to be defined for each sub-contract 'parcel' and entered for each sub-contract item. These codes allow the items for each sub-contractor to be collected together regardless of the page of the bill of quantities they originated from. They may then be incorporated in requests for quotations together with specification details (as described in Section 5.3.2 below). Using computer systems in this way significantly assists the process of obtaining quotations which, by traditional methods, involves photocopying relevant pages from bills of quantities (a task which is labour intensive, tedious and may be prone to errors).

    Notwithstanding the advantages of producing requests for sub-contract quotations in this manner, Brook (1995) sounds a word of caution. His concern is that this approach will result in sub-contractors considering items out of the context of other bill items and that this may result in claims at some later date. However, the bill pages normally sent to sub-contractors when manual procedures are used provide few additional bill items that set this context. The extent to which these fears are founded has therefore still to be assessed.

- *Materials quantities*   When bill items have been linked to suitable library build-ups, CAE systems may be used to calculate the total quantities of resources used in a bill of quantities. Thus, for example, these systems will calculate the total quantity of bricks arising from all brickwork items notwithstanding the fact that these may be scattered throughout a bill of quantities. Again, appreciable effort is required to arrive at these quantities using traditional methods.

CAE systems may thus be used to assist in the preparation of requests for quotations by collecting together similar items from throughout a bill and by calculating the total requirements for the resources used. This information may then be incorporated with 'Specifications' to provide a document which is sent to suppliers and sub-contractors.

5.3.2   Database of suppliers and sub-contractors

Several CAE systems provide facilities which allow estimators to store details relating to suppliers and sub-contractors (including addresses, phone and fax numbers as well as a rating of the particular supplier/sub-contractor's suitability for particular types of work). This makes it possible for requests for quotations (containing lists of bill items and/or resource quantities as described in Section 5.3.1) to be printed out and sent to selected suppliers and sub-contractors. In addition these data may also be linked with companies' quality assurance procedures which require ratings of suppliers' performance to be monitored and stored.

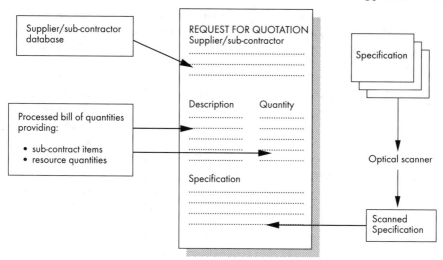

Figure 5.6   Flow chart of requests for quotations

5.3.3   Specifications

Enquiries to sub-contractors and materials suppliers also need to include specifications of the quality and workmanship required. To date, this area has attracted little interest from CAE system developers. Those responsible for 'tender buying' usually photocopy relevant pages from the tender specification and include them with other enquiry details. However, at least one major construction contractor views this area as sufficiently important to warrant the use of optical scanners. Relevant sections of a specification are scanned and the images produced are then linked with relevant item and resource quantities (described in Section 5.3.1 above). All these details are then printed out in the form of a request for a quotation. This process is illustrated in Figure 5.6.

It is worth noting that CITE (whose efforts to promote the electronic exchange of construction information are described in Section 2.5.2) are currently also encouraging building materials suppliers and contractors to use electronic channels of communication to transmit invoices. According to Cole (1995) it is conceivable that this medium of communication will be used for tender enquiries as both building merchants and contractors have expressed their interest in communicating in this way. In the United States some building materials merchants (as well as contractors, architects and other construction professionals) have started to advertise their wares and expertise via the Internet. The UK construction industry has been slow to respond to this approach even though it is possible to publish general price lists of materials in this way.

5.4   ANALYSING QUOTATIONS

Once suppliers (and/or sub-contractors) have submitted their quotations for a specific 'work package', estimators need to select one on which to base their estimate. To do this, they must ensure that all quotations are compared on the same basis and the *Code of Estimating Practice* (1983) provides a list of aspects to be checked in this connection. Amongst other factors, estimators need to take into account any discounts offered, and ensure that all quotations refer to the same bill items. It frequently occurs that some of the items (or resources) requested are not priced by one or more suppliers and the task of comparing quotations then becomes onerous. In these circumstances, CAE systems provide various facilities which help estimators allow for the costs of overcoming any discrepancies and divergences in the rates quoted. These include options which calculate average, highest and lowest costs based on item rates submitted by other suppliers. Brook (1995) cautions that this may be dangerous because 'in some systems the average changes when you add more sub-contract quotes. Estimators soon lose control. It is better if a sensible rate is inserted based on the level of pricing used by other sub-contractors.' When estimators have entered rates for all 'excluded' items, CAE systems compare quotations and highlight the most financially attractive option. Estimators may then exercise their judgement in selecting a supplier. This decision is frequently influenced by other aspects (such as the financial stability of a supplier, the supplier's reputation and so on) but computer-aided facilities are rarely used here.

In a similar vein, Turner (1995) advocates that estimators 'stand back from the computer with its screen by screen regime' at the time quotations are being analysed. He suggests that 'a print-out taken home in the evening and browsed through in front of the TV often highlights an anomaly or error not apparent from the screen'.

Once a selection has been made, costs (either for bill items or for resources) need to be transferred to the estimate files of a particular project. The facilities provided by CAE systems differ here as some require the selected rates to be re-entered into the system, whilst others allow these rates to be transferred automatically.

When CAE systems are used to prepare requests for quotations and to help in analysing the quotes received, they significantly assist in the estimating process.

5.5   REFINING ESTIMATING DATA

Item build-ups may be modified at any stage during the preparation of an estimate. Where these data have been extracted from an estimating library, it frequently occurs that production rates, wastage factors, the number of uses (on formwork materials), and user defined variables may need to be modified to reflect the particular requirements of an estimate. Equally, where item rates are built up from first principles (as described in Section 5.2.2), estimators frequently refine their calculations until they are satisfied that the most competitive result has been obtained. Part of this process of refining data involves updating the costs of resources, as already mentioned in Section 3.3. The facilities provided by CAE systems are key to this process.

One of the potential advantages of using a CAE system is that it allows various construction approaches to be costed before a final solution is decided upon. For example, estimators frequently need to evaluate the implications of placing concrete using different items of plant (e.g. a crane, a hoist or a pump). True, the costs of various alternatives may be calculated using manual methods, but the effort involved is onerous.

To make these changes using a CAE system alternative resources need to be selected and production rates altered as well. The ease with which these changes are effected depends largely on how estimating data have been structured and the facilities provided by CAE systems. One technique that assists in changing resources is the use of gangs (described in Section 3.5.2). To illustrate this, consider further the example of placing concrete. If estimators include 'concrete placing' gangs (containing labour and plant for one method of placing concrete) in all concrete items, the make-up of this gang may be altered (to reflect another method of placing), and this change will impact on all concrete items. Production rates may be changed by either increasing or decreasing the values stored in items or by using selective 'search and replace' facilities (if these are available). The key benefit of being able to ask (and answer) 'what if?' questions of CAE systems is dependent on these aspects. If these facilities are not exploited, estimators sacrifice a major attribute of the use of computer systems.

It is worth noting that all the changes that are made to library data create new, unique items and that these, in turn, may be stored for re-use with subsequent tenders. This is described in Section 3.3.

Over and above improving the iterative way in which estimates may be produced, CAE systems provide other approaches which may significantly influence the way in which estimates are produced. For example, once the items in bills of quantities have been linked to library build-ups it is possible, at a very early stage during the estimating process, to calculate the overall cost of a project (based on the production rates and resource costs held in the library). Various reports may then be produced to assist those preparing an estimate. These include:

- Reports which highlight those items that contribute significantly to the overall cost of a project. This is generally done by the CAE system re-arranging the order of bill items according to their total cost (rather than by the page on which the item appeared in the bill). This allows estimators to concentrate their efforts on these 'cost important' items.
- It is also possible to obtain reports of the total requirements for each of the resources used in the estimate. This information is not only useful to buyers (as described in Section 3.5.1) but also to planners who spend considerable time extracting these quantities from bills before preparing tender programmes.

These reports are indicative of the final costs and resource requirements of an estimate and are intended to give a 'feel' for a project.

5.6   PREPARING 'PRELIMINARIES'

CAE systems may be used to prepare the costs of 'Preliminaries' items, as the **resource based** library structure described in Section 3.3 may be used to cater for these data. However, few estimators choose to do this, preferring to use their own corporate checklists (similar to those recommended in the *Code of Estimating Practice* [1983]) either in hard copy form or as a computer spreadsheet. One of the main reasons for this is the fact that the Preliminaries items included in bills of quantities bear little resemblance to the way in which these costs are calculated by estimators. If CAE systems are used to prepare the costs of Preliminaries (by selecting resources and items from the Preliminaries section of an estimating library) these will inevitably conflict with the Preliminaries items presented in clients' bills of quantities. The approach adopted by most CAE users is to prepare Preliminaries costs using checklists and then to add these to the estimate amount provided by a CAE system. This works satisfactorily as it is only when a bill of quantities is called for by a client's representative (which usually occurs only when a contractor has submitted a potentially winning bid) that these costs need to be distributed to a bill of quantities.

Some CAE systems allow estimated costs to be allocated to durations of construction activities (prepared using computer-aided planning software) to produce forecasts of the expected cash flow for a project. Where Preliminaries have been prepared using checklists such as those described above, these costs need to be entered into a CAE system so that all costs for a project can be merged with activity durations. To achieve this in a way that is compatible with the rest of an estimate, Preliminaries costs need to be allocated to appropriate resource categories (e.g. labour, plant, transport, administrative costs and so on).

5.7   SUMMARY

This chapter has described the various ways in which estimates may be produced using a CAE system. The growing importance of obtaining and analysing quotations from sub-contractors and materials suppliers has also been highlighted as has the process of refining estimate data and estimating the costs of Preliminaries.

5.8   REFERENCES

Brook M (1995). Consultation with M Brook (FCIOB), Deputy Chairman, Procurement Committee, Chartered Institute of Building, October 1995.

Chartered Institute of Building (1983). *Code of estimating practice*, 5th Edition, ISBN 0906600650.

Cole T (1995). Consultation with T Cole, Managing Director, Interlock (Project Manager for CITE), October 1995.

Institution of Civil Engineers (1991). *Civil engineering standard method of measurement*, third edition, (CESSM3). Telford, ISBN 0727715615.

RICS/BEC (1988). *Standard method of measurement for building works, edition 7* (SMM7), (authorised by agreement between the Royal Institution of Chartered Surveyors and the Building Employers Confederation). Royal Institution of Chartered Surveyors, ISBN 0854063609.

Turner D (1995). Consultation with D Turner (FCIOB), member of CIOB Procurement Sub-Committee, October 1995.

CHAPTER 6

CONVERTING AN ESTIMATE INTO A TENDER AND ACTION WITH SUCCESSFUL TENDERS

6.1   SCOPE

The first part of this chapter describes the process of converting an estimate into a tender. This involves descriptions of the information which CAE systems provide and the adjustments and mark-ups which estimators and managers effect to arrive at a tender sum. When a tender is accepted by a client, estimators need to hand over estimate and tender details to those responsible for the construction of a project. The second part of this chapter describes the information that is made available to site personnel and how CAE systems can assist in facilitating this transfer of information. This chapter thus deals with the estimating and tendering process from the time an estimator completes an estimate until the time when a tender amount is finally agreed on.

6.2   INTRODUCTION

Tendering is defined in the *Code of Estimating Practice* (1983) as 'a separate and subsequent commercial function (to estimating that is) based upon the net cost estimate'. What information do those making these commercial decisions (hereafter referred to as 'management') require? The obvious answer is that they need details of all the costs likely to be incurred during the construction of a project. These details include documents which quantify and cost the construction work involved in a project (usually in the form of bills of quantities and, for the sake of clarity, referred to in this chapter as such) but other information, such as details of the locality and topography of a construction site, layout of the proposed site, availability of staff and so on is also required. At present computer systems are mainly used to help estimators calculate the anticipated costs of construction and little emphasis, if any, is placed on using these systems to assist management in visualising a project, the methods of construction proposed and so on. However, advances in CAD systems and the employment by contractors of staff trained to use these systems (resulting from the trend to construct projects on a 'design and build' basis) makes it likely that management may in future be presented with images which will help them in their review of construction costs. Gibb and Knobbs (1995) provide a useful review of progress in this area to date.

Plainly a bill of quantities is essential to the process of converting an estimate into a tender, but what form should this document take? Bills are provided by manual as well as computer-aided systems so what extra value does using a computer system bring to those adjudicating an estimate? A key advantage of CAE systems is that they can be used to summarise and re-arrange data to highlight areas where costs are concentrated. The rest of this section describes how CAE systems assist in this way.

6.2.1   Split bills of quantities

The **resource based** approach (described in Section 3.3) makes it possible for CAE systems to split item rates into whatever resource categories estimators choose (usually labour, plant, materials, sub-contractors and so on). Various reports and screen displays are provided, the most usual of which include split rates for:

- individual item rates
- the bill quantity of an item
- a range of bill items (such as a trade)
- a complete bill of quantities

These facilities mirror manual estimating methods, but release estimators from the drudgery of performing and checking these calculations.

6.2.2   Sorted bills of quantities

The sequence in which items are most frequently presented in bills of quantities is according to a standard method of measurement (e.g. SMM7, CESSM3). This arrangement makes no attempt to identify items which contribute significantly to the cost of a construction project. According to Bentley (1990), '10% of the items (in a bill of quantities) bear 90% of the value'. With very little effort CAE systems are able to highlight those bill items which contribute most of the costs in an estimate. Being able to identify these 'cost important' items not only allows estimators to 'concentrate on the most important items of work' (as described in Section 5.5) but also assists management in reviewing costs and assessing risks.

There are several ways in which cost important items may be identified. In the first instance some CAE systems simply allow bills to be presented in the order determined by the total cost of each bill item. With this approach the items of less cost significance are also presented and, as much of this information has little influence on the total cost of a project, it may be decided to dispense with these displays and/or print-outs at a certain point. Other CAE systems allow estimators to select a cost above (or below) which items are to be presented. Whatever method is used, the 'select and sort' facilities used by CAE systems allow estimators and management to make more effective use of their time by identifying those bill items which contribute disproportionately to the total cost of an estimate.

6.2.3   Resource reports

CAE systems produce reports of the total requirements and associated costs for the resources used in an estimate. This information may also be calculated manually, but the effort required to achieve it is generally considered prohibitive. As described in Section 3.5.1, resource costs and quantities are useful to many of those involved in preparing an estimate as well as to those converting an estimate into a tender. As shown in Figure 6.1, the order in which this information is produced usually follows the sequence of a bill of quantities and is frequently sub-totalled for each trade (or work section). However, this arrangement does not always provide estimators (and others involved in preparing an estimate, such as planners) with information in a suitable format. For example, some resources (such as labourers and cement) may be used in several trades of a bill as illustrated in Figure 6.2. Estimators wishing to refer to details of, for example, labourers involved in specific construction operations need to manipulate resource data further as described below.

- *Multiple resources*   This approach requires estimators to make several copies of the resources which occur in more than one trade (for example, 'OPC – brickwork', 'OPC – blockwork', 'OPC – concrete' and so on). Gangs and items then need to be assembled using appropriate resources (for example, mortar to be used for brickwork

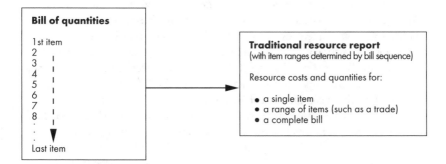

Figure 6.1   Traditional resource report

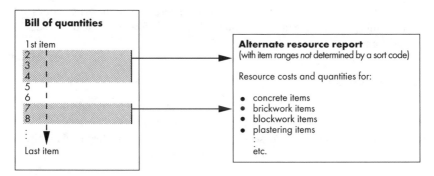

Figure 6.2   Alternative resource report

needs to be created using 'OPC – brickwork' as distinct from mortar for blockwork and so on). If this approach is consistently adopted, reports may be obtained which present resource costs and quantities for the construction operations required. This technique may prove satisfactory in some cases (such as housebuilding, where the make-up of items is likely to remain constant) but it does cause problems where the type of construction work tendered for is of a more varied nature. To warrant the effort required in developing an estimating library in this way, those using this approach need to be confident that bills of quantities still to be tendered for will be structured in a way that is compatible with the resource structure adopted. Rogue items (which will inevitably be encountered) may frustrate the implementation of this method. Secondly, this approach makes the collection of library items more complicated. Not only do estimators need to search through more data to find resources but gang rates also need to be copied (e.g. 'mortar – brickwork', 'mortar – blockwork' and so on). This proliferation of data causes the most serious disadvantage of this approach. When resource costs are revised, new rates need to be entered for each resource. Care needs to be taken to ensure that the costs for *all* copies of these multiple resources are revised as any omissions may obviously have serious consequences. Using multiple resources is effective in that it provides details for specific parts of a bill but it is also potentially dangerous.

■ *Sort codes*   The most elegant solution to this problem is to produce resource reports which are selected by some criterion other than bill item reference. However, not all CAE systems provide facilities which achieve this (and this is why the approaches described above are sometimes used). One of the techniques CAE systems use to extract this information is to include appropriate **item sort codes** (see Table 3.2) with bill items. These sort codes allow CAE systems to collect resources into defined categories (e.g. 'brickwork', 'concrete' and so on) and this information may then be presented for either a complete bill of quantities or for specified sections of it (see Figure 6.2). Some CAE systems provide **multiple sort codes** which enhance these system's capability for extracting resource data from specific sections of a bill of quantities. For example, if one sort code is used to define trades such as 'brickwork', 'concrete' and so on, and another sort code is used for specific locations within a building, it is possible to obtain reports which give resource details for 'brickwork in external works', 'brickwork in foundations' and so on. The CAE systems which provide these facilities generally make the entry and alteration of these **sort codes** relatively quick and simple to achieve thus making it possible to change these codes for each project tendered for.

6.2.4   Preliminaries

Management needs to consider the costs of Preliminaries items at tender adjudication stage. As described in Section 5.6 these are frequently assembled using manual or spreadsheet based checklists and consequently CAE systems are not often used in this connection unless forecasts of cash flow are required (see Section 5.6).

6.2.5   Average rates

The way in which resources and items may be arranged so that average rates can be calculated (for example, the average rate at which bricks are laid, or concrete is poured on a particular project) is described in Section 3.5.1. Being able to consider these rates is valuable to management as it allows them to make comparisons with previous estimates. Average rates may be calculated manually, but it is tedious to do so.

6.3   ADJUSTMENTS AND MARK-UPS

The *Code of Estimating Practice* (1983) suggests that the adjudication of a tender may entail 'two-tiered meetings', the first of which involves a review of an estimate, and a second at which the directorate of a construction company decides on a mark-up. Brook (1993) amplifies the content of these meetings by identifying the three main stages of this process as:

- understanding the nature and obligations of a project
- reviewing the costs given in an estimate, and if necessary, adjusting these costs according to market conditions
- adding to the estimate sums for general overheads and profit

Few computer aids are available to assist management in accomplishing the first task. As described in Section 6.2, the more widespread use of CAD may well play a part in this area in the future as may systems which assist in risk assessment. The need for the latter two aspects (i.e. a review of how an estimate has been built up and the addition of a mark-up) is reflected in the facilities CAE systems currently provide for this aspect of the estimating and tendering process. Essentially they involve **adjustment** facilities and **mark-up** facilities. The principle on which most of these facilities are based is that it should be possible to identify discrete sections of cost so that these may be manipulated according to market conditions, likely commercial advantage, risk and so on. CAE systems are able to extract and manipulate costs in this way but the manner in which estimating data are arranged may significantly influence how helpful these tendering facilities will be. These and other related aspects are described below.

6.3.1   Adjustments

As already mentioned in Section 5.5, the ability of CAE systems to quickly and accurately recalculate the costs of items based on alternative resource costs, production rates, wastage factors and so on is extremely attractive to estimators because it allows them to consider different methods of construction. This capability is usually exploited before tenders are adjudicated, but it is also sometimes used at adjudication meetings to allow management to assess the cost implications of any changes being considered. Where CAE systems are used to make alterations at this stage, caution needs to be exercised to keep track of any changes that are made. Where several alterations are made (some of which may be changes to changes), it is possible to lose track of the starting

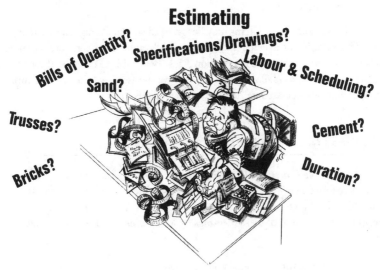

Figure 6.3   A disciplined approach to adjusting estimate costs is essential

point. There is much that estimators and management need to accomplish at adjudication meetings and some feel that CAE systems hinder rather than help when used to make adjustments at adjudication meetings (in fact at least one construction company bans their use at these meetings and makes all necessary adjustments on print-outs). Whilst this view may seem extreme, it emphasises the importance of a disciplined approach to adjusting estimate costs (and, presumably, reflects the confusion that may result when this is not done).

6.3.2   Mark-ups

Can CAE systems help management in making the commercial decisions required to convert estimates into tenders? Tah et al (1994) have observed that this area of estimating 'involves management decisions that are highly subjective, involving qualitative information that is often vague and difficult to structure and quantify'. Fayek et al (1994) found in a recent survey of seventeen estimating systems, that 'the analysis and decision-making process required in tendering is largely unrepresented in computerised form'. CAE systems can assist in marking up bills of quantities and do so in a wide variety of different ways. However, Fayek's observations refer to more esoteric tendering aids such as those which assist in assessing the 'inherent risks and opportunities in the project, market conditions, competitors tendering for the same project, company need for the work, company experience, project complexity, and desired profit'. Tah et al (1994) found that 'statistical and probabilistic methods were considered too difficult, too time consuming, and expensive to implement' in this connection. It is plain that this relatively undocumented area of tendering is ripe for further development and is currently being investigated by, amongst others, Tah et al (1994). However, the competitive nature of tendering has impeded the publication of

research in this area, and will probably do so in the foreseeable future. Few textbooks
and papers are available on the ways in which mark-ups may be applied and what the
implications of applying such mark-ups in a specific manner are likely to be. This lack of
published information is due to the commercial nature and confidentiality of the
decisions taken at this time (Tah et al [1994]). Many of those making these decisions
consider that their tendering approach provides advantages over competitors and are
therefore fearful of this information becoming common knowledge.

Notwithstanding these difficulties, it is likely that some construction companies will
exploit the ever increasing power of computer systems to develop programs which assist
in making better informed decisions at this time. Whether or not specialist programs
such as these will become widely accepted by the construction industry is a matter of
speculation. In the past, approaches with which estimators were not familiar have been
tried without success. For example, in the late 1970s and early 1980s contractors were
encouraged, unsuccessfully, to use regression analysis (a statistical approach used, in this
context, to predict tender prices based on those of past tenders) for estimating. Despite
the encouraging results produced by this research, regression has never been accepted as
an estimating method suitable for the construction industry. This is not to say that
innovative methods will not be used by some contractors. In any field there are pioneers,
but their approaches are likely to be guarded closely.

Most CAE systems provide several different ways of marking up estimates. These
have evolved in response to users' requirements and are sufficiently general in nature not
to be viewed as commercially sensitive (and therefore confidential). An analysis of these
facilities arguably provides an insight to the strategies and manipulations that
management uses to convert estimates into tenders. However, in the section below no
attempt has been made to analyse the tendering strategies which underlie these facilities
as such an examination is outside the scope of this book.

Whether or not these facilities are actually used during tender adjudication meetings
depends on the procedures adopted by individual companies. As described in Section
6.3.1, some estimators and managers prefer to make changes manually. Where this is the
case, mark-up facilities such as those described below are only used when bills of
quantities are called for by clients' representatives (see Section 6.4.1).

Tender mark-up facilities may be divided into those which address resources and
those which affect items. In both cases CAE systems treat mark-up as an additional
component of an item rate (i.e. item cost + mark-up = item price).

- *Resource mark-ups*   Those responsible for finalising tenders may wish to apply
  different mark-ups to labour, plant, materials, sub-contract resources and, where
  estimators have defined their own resource categories, to these resources as well. The
  resource reports referred to in Section 6.2.3 provide management with a starting
  point for assessing the importance and risk associated with these resources and for
  manipulating cash flow (see also 'Front and back end loading' at the end of this
  section). Mark-ups may then be applied to a complete resource category, or to a sub-
  set. A coherent and well structured coding system (as described in Section 4.3.2)
  makes the selection of these sub-sets of resources easy to accomplish and further
  emphasises the importance of well structured coding systems.

Resources are usually marked up on a percentage basis with most CAE systems catering for negative as well as positive mark-ups. In addition, some systems allow management to add (or deduct) sums of money to categories of resources. In these cases the sums of money are usually evenly distributed over a selected range of resources.

- *Item mark-ups*   The facilities which allow items to be marked up are similar to those described for resources above. Many CAE systems provide facilities which allow management to either mark up (or mark down) all the items contained in a bill of quantities or a particular range of bill items. This is usually achieved by applying a percentage mark-up but frequently additional facilities are provided which allow sums of money to be added to (or deducted from) ranges of items as well.

- *Gang mark-ups*   The facilities for marking up gangs are generally the same as those for resources and items and depend on the approach adopted by each CAE system for storing these data (see Section 3.5.2).

- *Resource, gang and item mark-ups*   Most CAE systems allow resource and item mark-ups to be applied in virtually any combination within the same estimate as shown in Figure 6.4. In such cases it is possible for management to, for example, reduce the costs of all materials by one per cent and to add three per cent to all earthworks items.

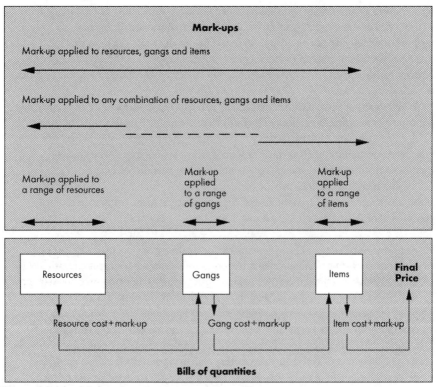

Figure 6.4   Applying mark-ups to resources, gangs and items

- *Final sums*   The facilities described above are helpful in arriving at a final tender amount. However, on occasions management may decide on a final tender sum and the balancing figure (i.e. the difference between the estimate cost and the tender sum agreed on) needs to be distributed over the items in a bill of quantities as mark-up. Where these facilities are available, this balancing figure may be either positive or negative and may be spread over a range of bill items or all items in a bill of quantities.
- *Front and back end loading*   Although publicly frowned upon by most contractors, some CAE systems provide facilities which allow management to attempt to improve their company's cash flow by increasing the mark-up applied to certain ranges of bill items. Such loading can be dangerous as observed by Turner (1995) 'especially when applied to provisional items which may in the final analysis be reduced thus losing a disproportionate amount of mark-up'. The mechanisms by which this is achieved vary from system to system. Essentially a sum of money is defined as a mark-up amount and this is then distributed over specified ranges of bill items. Some systems allow the mark-up on certain items to be increased whilst at the same time the mark-up on all other items is decreased pro rata. The bill total thus remains the same but mark-up moneys are unevenly distributed within these bills of quantities. Items which attract this 'loaded' mark-up include items built early in the construction process in the case of front-end loading, and late in this process with back-end loading. The extent to which these facilities are actually used in practice is uncertain as anecdotal evidence (the only source of reference) is sparse.

6.4   ACTION WITH SUCCESSFUL TENDERS

Most construction companies submit several tenders for every one they win. When they are successful, a new phase of the CAE process starts. With building projects this firstly involves submitting a priced bill of quantities to a client's representative. Following this, details of the estimate need to be passed to those responsible for monitoring and controlling the costs of construction. The process with civil engineering tenders is slightly different as priced bills of quantities usually need to be submitted at the time of tender and the sequence of activities described below is necessarily different.

6.4.1   Preparing bills of quantities for submission to clients

The success rate in winning tenders for building work varies, but one in ten may well be considered average in current market conditions. Estimators and management naturally try to avoid unnecessary tendering costs wherever possible and this may influence the way in which estimates are prepared when CAE systems are used. A compounding factor is that the time available to prepare estimates is limited and estimators frequently take short-cuts to enable them to meet tender deadlines. These short-cuts range from the trivial (such as entering spot rates for cost unimportant items), to those which are more significant (such as entering sub-contract quotations as a lump sum instead of entering individual item rates). The need to translate these short-cuts into a more intelligible format is generally only addressed when bills of quantities are requested by clients' representatives as a bill, once called for and accepted by a client's quantity surveyor, becomes a legally binding document. With most building tenders, this only occurs after the official opening of tenders. (As already mentioned, the norm for civil engineering projects is for priced bills of quantities to be submitted as part of a tender.)

Estimators need to ensure that:

- The costs of 'Preliminaries' items are apportioned appropriately to the items contained in a bill of quantities (see Section 5.6).
- All the adjustments decided on at tender adjudication meetings are made to the data concerned. In Section 6.3.1 it was noted that some estimators and managers prefer to calculate adjustments manually at these meetings. Where this is so, estimating data need to be altered so that CAE bills of quantities reflect the decisions taken.
- Where lump sum sub-contract quotations have previously been entered, individual item rates are entered for each bill item.
- Mark-up is distributed according to decisions of management. As described in Section 6.3.2, mark-ups are sometimes added manually during tender adjudication meetings. These need to be spread over estimating data (in the various ways described in Section 6.3.2).

Once all these additions and/or changes have been completed, priced bills of quantities need to be submitted to clients' quantity surveyors. However, quantity surveyors have a wide variety of attitudes to bills of quantities prepared by CAE systems. Some accept documents that are printed by these systems whilst others insist that item rates are manually written into a bill. The use of electronic bills of quantities (EBQs), described in Section 2.5, has met with a muted response as have programmed EBQs (described in Section 2.6). In many cases contractors are required to relegate the use of their computer systems to a support role so that the age-old task of 'inking in' rates into a bill of quantities can be completed.

In summary, CAE systems assist estimators both in refining estimate costs and in entering mark-ups. Some quantity surveyors encourage contractors to submit bills of quantities prepared by CAE systems, and an enlightened few recognise the benefits of receiving this data in an electronic form as well as a printed document. However, the current state of computer awareness in the construction industry is such that it is likely to be a considerable time before this attitude becomes widespread.

6.4.2   Preparing details for site management

In addition to the aspects noted in Section 6.4.1 above (which are usually completed before details of a project are passed to site management) a further recommendation is that all assumptions made during the preparation of an estimate are recorded using resource and items comments facilities (where these are provided by CAE systems – see Table 3.1 and Table 3.2). The underlying theme is to provide site managers with details of all the decisions taken in preparing an estimate and converting it to a tender so that they may successfully manage their project.

The importance of CAE systems to this phase of the construction process is aptly described by Brook (1993) as follows: 'Gone are the days when the award of a contract signalled the end of the estimator's contribution to a project. There are two important tasks to be performed: first, helping the construction team with procurement and technical advice during the mobilisation period, and second, producing cost information which will form the budget for the job. The transfer of information has been improved considerably with the introduction of computers. There are many estimating packages available which can be used to produce tender allowances and later assist during the construction phase to control sub-contractors' payments and produce valuations for the client.'

A discussion on the computer applications that make use of estimate and tender data is outside the scope of this book. However, as illustrated in Figure 1.2, these data are extremely valuable when computer systems are used to prepare interim valuations for the construction work completed on site. Implicit in this is the presumption that the data stored for a particular project reflect the final decisions and alterations required by the management of a construction company as well as those resulting from any post-tender adjustments required by clients' quantity surveyors.

6.5 SUMMARY

This chapter has highlighted the fact that CAE systems provide estimate data which are not feasible to obtain using manual estimating approaches. These data are invaluable in helping those adjudicating an estimate in making their decisions regarding adjustments and mark-up. It has also described the various ways in which these tender adjustments and mark-ups may be applied and concluded with a brief description of the factors that need to be considered when a bill of quantities is submitted to a client's quantity surveyor, and when estimate and tender details are provided to those responsible for the construction process.

6.6 REFERENCES

Bentley J I W (1990). *Construction tendering and estimating*. E & F N Spon, ISBN 0419142401.

Brook M (1993). *Estimating and tendering for construction work*. Butterworth Heinemann, ISBN 0750615311.

Chartered Institute of Building (1983). *Code of estimating practice*, 5th Edition. ISBN 0906600650.

Fayek A, Duffield C F and Young D M (1994). A review of commercially available cost-estimating software systems for the construction industry. *Engineering Management Journal*, Vol. 6, No. 4, 4 December.

Gibb A G F and Knobbs T (1995). Computer-aided site layout and facilities planning. Association of Researchers in Construction Management, eleventh annual conference. York, September 1995. Vol. 2.

Institution of Civil Engineers (1991). *Civil engineering standard method of measurement*, third edition, (CESSM3). Telford, ISBN 0727715615.

RICS/BEC (1988). *Standard method of measurement for building works*, edition 7 (SMM7), (authorised by agreement between the Royal Institution of Chartered Surveyors and the

Building Employers Confederation). Royal Institution of Chartered Surveyors, ISBN 0854063609.

Tah J H M, Thorpe A and McCaffer R (1994). A survey of indirect cost estimating practice. *Construction Management and Economics*, Vol. 12, No. 1, January. ISSN 0144-6193.

Turner D (1995). Consultation with D Turner (FCIOB), member of CIOB Procurement Sub-Committee, October 1995.

CHAPTER 7

TRAINING TO USE COMPUTER-AIDED ESTIMATING SYSTEMS

7.1 SCOPE

Competent staff are essential for the efficient operation of computer systems. CAE systems are no exception and this chapter describes some of the approaches adopted in training estimators. It addresses four fundamental questions, i.e. what do estimators need to know, where should they be trained, and how and when should this be done?

7.2 INTRODUCTION

Estimators come from many different backgrounds. Some progress through the trades, completing a diploma or degree (either on a part time or a full time basis) and working on a construction site, or gaining experience in some other construction related discipline. This wide range of possible backgrounds has one common aspect – few estimators are likely to have received any formal education in the use of computer systems and even fewer a theoretical background to the use of construction software. Anecdotal evidence suggests that most estimators teach themselves a lot of what they know about computer systems and have learned this by trial and error and/or by attending various short courses on topics that interest them. However, estimators are often expected to have a detailed knowledge and appreciation of computer systems. This has arisen due to the increased use of computer systems generally and the increased sophistication of CAE systems in particular. There is plainly a mismatch between the training estimators receive and the knowledge and expertise they are expected to have.

When construction companies invest in CAE systems, the main costs generally considered are hardware and software. Seldom is serious consideration given to the cost of training, but this essential activity needs to be taken into account because the sums of money involved may be appreciable. Not only is there the obvious cost of paying software vendors for training, but there is the cost of unproductive time of estimators to consider (both whilst they are learning how to use the system and also during the 'learning curve' they experience before they become proficient users). Training can be a considerable cost when installing a computer system and this needs to be recognised.

(According to Harrison (1995), if a planned approach to training is not implemented, the time wasted by staff learning how to use systems inefficiently is likely to cost even more!). When the feasibility of installing a CAE system is being considered, those involved frequently attempt to justify expenditure in terms of savings that may be made due to increased estimating efficiency, but this is difficult to accomplish. Many companies set themselves efficiency targets, but few have the experience of actually training staff and installing computer systems to base these calculations on anything more than a good guess. The decision to invest in CAE systems is seldom made on the basis of expected financial advantages.

The fact that estimators need to be trained and that training costs money is indisputable. However, there are many different approaches to providing this training which need to be assessed before a particular route is adopted. This chapter focuses on four main questions, i.e. what knowledge should estimators have, where is this best obtained, and how and when should it be taught?

7.3   WHAT DO ESTIMATORS NEED TO KNOW?

Computer systems include both physical components (i.e. hardware) and programs (i.e. operating system software, application software and so on). The functions of both need to be understood to appreciate how computer systems operate and how they are used in the work place. The relative emphasis on these aspects is likely to be different depending on whether those being trained are students or whether they have been working for some time.

7.3.1   Teaching students

The bodies which accredit construction courses (the Chartered Institute of Building (CIOB) and the Royal Institution for Chartered Surveyors (RICS)), provide some guidance on what should be taught. The CIOB's *Education and Professional Development Manual* (1994) sets out this Institute's requirements for its members. It requires computer systems to be introduced at an early stage and that students should:

- Have an appreciation of computer systems which incorporates an overview of these systems with an emphasis on personal computer equipment. They should be familiar with computer terminology and should be able to recognise the use of databases for storage and retrieval of data.
- Be aware of health and safety legislation affecting visual display screens.
- Be introduced to the development of electronic spreadsheet models for the solution of building problems.
- Have an appreciation of applications packages and experience of the operation of commercial packages currently available for the building industry.

The CIOB and RICS recommend broadly the same exposure to computers for their members. However, one area that is the subject of debate notwithstanding these recommendations is whether or not students should develop skills in writing computer programs. In the past some computer courses have placed heavy emphasis on this aspect but is it relevant in today's world? Progress over the past ten years has so changed the world of computing that this view is strongly questioned by most lecturers involved in this area. Increasingly, the consensus is that more emphasis should be placed on students becoming familiar with 'off-the-shelf' computer packages than with learning a computer language. Arguments in favour of this approach include:

- Excellent computer programs already exist so why prepare students to re-invent the wheel?
- The time available for students to learn about computers is limited. How can they become proficient in a computer language in the time available?
- Increasingly the trend is for construction companies to use 'off-the-shelf' packages rather than develop their own. With this in mind, will graduates who cannot write computer programs be at any disadvantage?
- Will students ever use these skills outside a university environment?
- Many of the problems that students will face on graduation are likely to be able to be solved using either a spreadsheet or a database program. Recognising this, what advantage will the knowledge of a computer language provide?

Those who disagree include academics who feel that teaching a computer language (such as BASIC) enables students to use packages (particularly spreadsheets and databases) better as the macro languages used in these packages use the same syntax as BASIC. Some lecturers are also worried that standards will be lowered if students do not master a subject more demanding than the use of application software. In addition, the argument that students should be able to write computer programs appears to be based on past practices (probably originating in civil engineering departments, where an ability to prepare FORTRAN programs was seen as an essential part of a student's education). This has not been proved relevant to the requirements of those likely to be employed as estimators and quantity surveyors. Practitioners and academics generally agree that a working knowledge of general and construction related programs is of prime importance to this job function.

The CIOB recognises the impact that computer systems and the management of information have on commercial organisations. It is conscious of the fact that computer systems should not be taught in isolation and, according to Baldwin (1995), its Computing and Information Technology sub-committee recommends that subjects which form part of CIOB accredited courses deal, where appropriate, with the use of computer systems as an integral part of the syllabus concerned. Furthermore, Miller and Young (1995) recommend in a CIOB publication that educators should be encouraged 'to ensure that students are told about such aids in every aspect of their studies so that they see a computer as an information processor similar to an aggregate and cement processor: it does the job better than pen or shovel'. A draft syllabus is being prepared by the Computing and Information Technology sub-committee which should allow students to specialise in the area of information technology in their final year of studies. The emphasis of this subject is likely to be on the management of information within the context of a construction company.

According to Landor (1995), the RICS similarly 'recognises the importance which computing and the management of information has had on commercial organisation and practice'. He states that ' . . . the Institution would expect that information technology should permeate all aspects of teaching and delivery of programme. Students should have exposure to a variety of software applications appropriate to the Surveying discipline being taught . . .'.

Inevitably the requirements of the accrediting bodies are interpreted differently by colleges and universities. The CIOB recognises differences which occur as a reflection of the individual nature of these institutions. It furthermore encourages universities to promote and develop their own strengths and, provided the subject matter falls within the scope defined in their *Education and Professional Development Manual*, will accredit such courses. This approach is also endorsed by the RICS.

7.3.2   Training experienced estimators

What about estimators who have received no formal computer education? Clearly they need a different programme of training to that described in Section 7.3.1 above. In common with people in similar positions in other industries, they are frequently apprehensive about learning to use computer systems. They feel ill-equipped to use a computer keyboard, and are generally fearful that their lack of understanding of computer systems will open them to ridicule by their more computer-literate peers. Those developing training programmes for such estimators need to be conscious of these feelings and develop courses that build on strengths rather than expose weaknesses. One strategy that has been used successfully is to concentrate on using a CAE system and to place little emphasis on the workings of computer systems (certainly during the early stages of training). There are several reasons for this:

- Estimators generally need little or no knowledge of operating systems when they start using a CAE system. Similarly, hardware constraints and other related concepts mean little to estimators until they are able to relate these to producing an estimate.
- In all training situations it is important for participants to feel that they are making progress. This is particularly important for this group as failure to grasp and apply concepts may quickly turn to a general non-acceptance of computer systems. Interest is likely to be maintained where relevant tasks, such as different ways of analysing sub-contractor quotations, different ways of building up item rates and so on are explained. Esoteric aspects of working with computer systems (such as formatting diskettes, making backups, memory optimisation, disk management and so on) may then be introduced as necessary incidentals of using this technology rather than aspects of prime importance.

Experience has shown that CAE training courses structured in this way are more likely to result in motivated estimators than those which concentrate on aspects of computer technology. This strategy recognises the fact that some estimators may eventually need to know more about operating systems, hardware and so on.

This section has concentrated on training experienced estimators new to CAE and computer systems. Clearly training needs to be tailored to specific requirements and should allow those interested to increase and develop their understanding.

7.4 WHEN SHOULD ESTIMATORS BE TRAINED?

The obvious answer to this is as young as possible. Most educators agree that computer systems should be integrated into general education from an early age. The rationale behind this is that computers should be just another tool to be used in everyday life. Computer systems abound, and there is little doubt that the younger generation have benefited from exposure to computer systems as they are not as intimidated by the technology as their elders. Parents who expose their children to computers through computer games, CD-ROM encyclopaedias, access to the Internet and so on are laying a foundation of computer awareness that may be built on in later years.

However, it is never too late to learn and there are many estimators who have become avid users of computer systems late in their working life. There are also some who say that, whilst computer technology and CAE systems provide appreciable benefits, they should only be installed 'on my retirement'. There will always be those who are not comfortable using computer systems but seeking to identify and classify this group of people by age is not valid.

What is to happen in the meantime? It will be many years before the majority of trainee estimators have had the benefit of an education which introduced them to computer systems as tools for everyday use. A strategy for training those new to estimating in the use of these systems is required now. Equally important is the issue of re-training estimators not familiar with CAE systems in the use of this technology and updating this knowledge from time to time.

7.4.1 Training those new to estimating

As suggested above, estimators of the future are likely to begin their formal computer education at school. Those who continue to higher education in the United Kingdom will then be exposed to more theory and practise relating to computers (an example of the work that some university students complete is described in the Appendix). Most programmes of study are arranged in such a way that students reinforce their general background in computers during their first year studies and then move on to estimating in subsequent years of study. The use of CAE systems is generally seen as supplementary to the estimating subjects taught on these courses.

Not all estimators progress through university or college and there are a variety of routes that qualify them for this vocation (such as NVQs, and the CIOB 'direct entry' exams). These programmes of study generally deal with computers in a similar manner to most higher education courses, i.e. students first learn the basics about computer systems and then progress to more advanced topics after a grounding in the theory of other construction subjects has been attained.

Should those training to become estimators learn first about computer systems and then about estimating or vice versa? As there have been no formal studies to establish the relative merits of these two approaches, educationalists and construction companies wishing to base their education and training strategy on accepted best practice are left to their past experience and prejudices. The traditional view is to ensure trainee estimators obtain a thorough understanding of building up item rates, labour, plant, materials, sub-contractors and so on *before* starting to use CAE systems. However, some argue that this approach is outdated and that estimators should learn by making use of modern tools rather than employing methods that have their roots in outdated manual procedures. Others are critical of this approach and draw an analogy with knowing how to use a tool (e.g. a bricklayer's trowel). This knowledge helps bricklayers lay bricks but it does not mean that these will be laid in a way that best contributes to the overall performance of a building. Thus knowing how to use a CAE system does not mean that estimates will be produced in the most efficient way and herein lies the dilemma. CAE systems provide many different approaches and a thorough understanding of the *principles* of estimating is essential if an informed assessment of the merits of each method is to be made. Those who are not familiar with these principles may be tempted to accept the first process they become familiar with. The traditional approach of learning about an application and then using computer systems to ease any manual drudgery associated with it thus appears to be the most suitable training strategy.

Once estimators have completed their formal education many of them are likely to have access to CAE systems when they start full time employment. (According to a recent CICA survey (1993), 'Computers are now used for estimating in 79% of contractors' offices'.) However, there is little likelihood that the CAE system used at college or university will be the same as that provided by an employer. Sceptics may argue that this negates the effort spent in learning how to use these systems. The converse is more likely to be true. Familiarity with various CAE systems enables estimators to identify differences in estimating approach and nuances between systems. This should lead to a more efficient use of these systems as proficiency in using a CAE system is an amalgam of computer awareness, estimating expertise, and a determination to get the job done. The more opportunities estimators have had to question different approaches, the more likely they are to be able to use systems to their best advantage.

7.4.2   Re-training estimators

As already mentioned, estimators come from all walks of life and bring with them a wide spectrum of both computer knowledge and estimating expertise. It is obvious that those who have had formal computer training are likely to adapt to CAE systems more readily than those who have had none. However, many have had little exposure to computers and even less to CAE systems. Similarly some estimators may have learnt on one system and subsequently be required to work on another. Clearly all will benefit from a planned programme of training. Suggestions for the contents of these sessions are provided in Section 7.6.

7.4.3   Continuing professional development

Most professional institutions (including the CIOB and RICS) and employers support the concept of continuing professional development (CPD). Estimators need to attend these events and update their knowledge and skills on a continual basis. Seminars and short courses are to be encouraged in this regard. However, many of the estimating functions that are arranged are sometimes seen as opportunities for software vendors to sell their products. In a specialist area such as estimating and with computer technology developing as quickly as it currently is, it can be argued that this is indeed an effective way for estimators to keep informed of current developments.

7.5 WHERE SHOULD TRAINING BE GIVEN?

Education is an on-going process and estimators currently starting employment are likely to have learnt about computer systems from an early stage. In an ideal world they would have grown so familiar with this technology by the time they reach a contractor's office that they see computers as a part of their every day life and use these systems just like any other tool.

7.5.1   At school

It is common knowledge that many children feel more at ease with computer technology than their parents. This is due in no small part to the availability of computer systems at schools, in the home and generally in the environment to which they are exposed. In this context, playing computer games may be seen to play a positive role as this activity contributes to the ease with which children learn how to use new programs and know how to interact with these systems. There are certainly some children who, like some adults, are technophobic and avoid using computers wherever possible. No data are available on how this affects estimators, but Harrison (1995) notes that ' . . . with around 800 systems supplied, we have only heard of one estimator being so technophobic as to be unable to use a computer'. People who do not want to use computer systems provide a challenge to educational establishments (as well as to employers) to provide them with opportunities to develop skills and strategies necessary to use these systems effectively.

7.5.2   At college or university

The estimators of the future should be using computer systems as part of their every day life by the time they reach higher education. That this is not the case is patently obvious to many lecturers who provide opportunities for students to give evidence of such expertise. This is why many construction courses provide introductory computing subjects which serve as a refresher to computer literate students and act as a primer to others. A knowledge and understanding of computer systems is an essential facet of construction education and is provided by those higher education institutions accredited by the CIOB and RICS.

7.5.3   On the job

There are many advantages to training estimators to use CAE systems in a work environment. These aspects are described below and are similar for most computer applications.

- In many cases estimators are likely to use their own computer system when in-house training is given. This makes it possible for the examples completed at this time to be retained on estimators' computers and reviewed at a later stage. This may also be done by copying data onto a disk and transferring it to another computer system but it rarely occurs when training is given at remote locations. Being able to review what was done once training has been completed supports learning and is to be encouraged.
- Training takes place in familiar surroundings and those participating are likely to experience few distractions resulting from a new environment (though the converse may be argued, i.e. different surroundings may contribute to better concentration).
- Training which occurs at a place of work is likely to be cost effective as a single trainer can teach several staff (though probably not more than ten), rooms and computers are likely to be available, there will be no extra transport and subsistence costs for staff attending the course and so on.

There are some disadvantages to training estimators at a place of work. These include:

- Staff being easily distracted (e.g. to attend to their everyday job). This is probably the most serious problem associated with this approach.
- The facilities that staff work in may not be suitable for training. For example, to be cost effective, several staff will need to be taught at the same time and rooms large enough to accommodate the number of persons and their computer systems will be required. Depending upon the availability of rooms, staff may have to be taught in surroundings not suited to learning.

7.5.4   At short courses

Software vendors sometimes arrange short courses at which estimators and related staff from various construction organisations come together. Where these functions are arranged for training purposes, they provide a cost effective solution whilst avoiding the disadvantages described in Section 7.5.3. However, the competitive and strategic nature of estimating is such that estimators seldom feel at ease when their rivals are present. As the participants in these training sessions generally work individually or in small groups, this rivalry naturally inhibits learning. Participants are hesitant to pose and answer questions that might be interpreted by others as a corporate estimating strategy. Where training short courses are delivered, they are usually arranged solely for a particular organisation. There is little doubt that estimators could benefit from discussing their experiences with other estimators. Where this discussion takes place it usually does so within individual organisations. It is unfortunate that the nature of estimating is not conducive to sharing experiences of CAE.

7.6   HOW SHOULD ESTIMATORS BE TRAINED?

There are many different ways in which estimators may learn how to use their CAE system. The different methods described below provide an indication of the variety of approaches that may be encountered.

7.6.1 Self taught

Training costs prompt many construction companies to organise training in-house and this frequently involves estimators teaching themselves how to use a CAE system. The various ways in which this may be achieved include working through tutorial exercises (if these have been provided with the system), reading through user manuals (if they are available), or simply learning by trial and error.

The costs of training by this approach may appear minimal as estimators are expected to learn how to use these systems in addition to performing their day to day tasks. Just how much time needs to be spent depends on many factors. Most computer users expect to able to operate their system intuitively. Whilst this may be possible with some popular general purpose programs, the market for construction software is limited and CAE developers generally do not have the expected turnover or resources to provide the same functionality as, say, Microsoft Excel. Estimators expecting the same ease of use, printing options and so on with their CAE system as they are used to with, for example, spreadsheets may be disappointed. The fact of the matter is that CAE systems can be more difficult to use than modern general purpose computer programs.

In addition, the low sales volume nature of the construction market means that CAE developers are generally forced to spend less money on user documentation, help screens and so on than with high sales volume programs. The documentation provided with a CAE system varies from paper-based manuals to those which are supplied on disk to be printed out (as and when required). The quality of user documentation varies from system to system. On-line help facilities are provided with most CAE systems though the ease with which these may be used (and the relevance of the advice given) varies between systems.

Estimators who train themselves may eventually become proficient users of their CAE systems. However, those who are serious about using these systems effectively should recognise that leaving estimators to their own devices is a potentially risky and possibly costly training strategy.

7.6.2 Courses provided by software vendor

Many of the advantages and disadvantages of this approach have already been described in Sections 7.5.3 and 7.5.4. Where these are well organised and form part of a coherent training strategy they are effective.

7.6.3 One to one training with software vendor

Having someone available to answer questions is reassuring to learners, but whether this is a cost effective way of learning how to use computer systems is not so certain. CAE system vendors have different approaches to charging for training costs. Some provide assistance as and when required but make a charge for all time spent by their staff. Others rent their software and provide training and support (as well as updates to their software) as part of their rental agreement. These are probably extremes and many variations in the way contractors are charged for training by software vendors no doubt exist. However, the fact remains that training one person at a time must be expensive and should be considered a luxury rather than a favoured approach.

The truth of the matter is that there is no substitute for getting 'one's hands dirty' and learning oneself. This is not to advocate the 'self-taught' approach described in Section 7.6.1 but underscores the importance of reinforcing the effort put in at training sessions. Unless estimators put into practice what they have learnt at these times they are sure to forget and may then be tempted to call their software vendor. This is all very well if there is no cost involved but this is seldom the case.

7.6.4   Self taught with access to 'hot line' support

As mentioned in Section 7.6.3, there are many different ways in which CAE vendors provide support to users of their systems. One valuable service is a telephone 'hot-line' which estimators may phone for advice and help. Many estimators who learn how to use their CAE system themselves use this service frequently. However, the cost of providing this support (and no doubt the trivial nature of some calls made by new users) has prompted some organisations to rationalise the ways this is provided. An interesting approach is that adopted by Microsoft for supporting its Windows 95 operating system. Ninety days worth of support is provided free of charge and, once this period has elapsed, callers are charged for help. According to Samson (1995) 'probably the most important fact for the new user to bear in mind is that the free 90-day warranty does not begin until the first support call is made . . . It means it is very much in users' own interest to try to solve problems without reaching automatically for the telephone.' This highlights the fact that 'hot-line' support is generally seen as an efficient way of assisting users. However, to be cost effective it should only be used when other cheaper avenues of support (such as help screens and user manuals) have been exhausted.

7.6.5   Peer tutoring

Another approach that may be used to advantage is to learn from someone else in an organisation. The benefits of 'peer' tutoring (the jargon educationalists use for this method) include the fact that those learning do so at their own pace, whilst those teaching have a chance to consider alternative ways of performing various tasks. These benefits extend beyond simply being an efficient way of teaching and learning. 'Team building', an aspect so important in construction companies, is also encouraged.

7.7   SUMMARY

This chapter has identified the computer-related topics that students are likely to learn at school and during higher education as well as those which experienced estimators need to address. It has described the stages of career development at which estimators may be trained as well as where this should occur. It concluded by looking at the various methods by which estimators may be taught how to use CAE systems. In summary there are many ways in which each of these aspects may be achieved but there are no all-encompassing solutions – each case needs to be considered on its merits.

7.8 REFERENCES

Baldwin A N B (1995). (Member of CIOB Computing and Information Technology Sub-Committee), August 1995.

CIOB (1994). *Education and professional development manual.*

Harrison R (1995). Consultation with R Harrison (FCIOB), Managing Director, Manifest Systems Ltd, October 1995.

Landor E (1995). Consultation with E Landor, Head of Education and Training, The Royal Institution of Chartered Surveyors, September 1995.

Miller P and Young D (1995). IT watch. In *Focus professional services and education.* CIOB, ISBN 3808904078.

Samson J (1995). If stuck, read the manual. Windows 95 Supplement to *The Times*, 24 August.

The Construction Industry Computing Association (CICA) and KPMG Peat Marwick (1993). *Building on IT – for quality.* ISBN 0906225191.

TEACHING COMPUTING APPLICATIONS

A.1 SCOPE

This book has been written for practising estimators as well as students in construction related disciplines and their tutors. It is to the latter that this appendix is addressed. Those teaching construction related topics have very few opportunities to find out how their colleagues at other institutions deliver their subject material. One of the few opportunities to interact in this way has been the Department of Employment's recent Discipline Network initiative and seminar (reported in *Construction Manager* [1995]). This provided a unique forum for academics to share their views on 'best practice' and was widely commended by representatives of the CIOB accredited courses present. The aim of this appendix is to continue this initiative by providing details of one approach to teaching university students how computer systems may be used in the construction industry.

Throughout this chapter the term **student** has been used to include the various different categories of person involved in learning about computer systems (for example, those involved in construction management, building, quantity surveying, civil engineering, mature students and so on).

A.2 HOW IS COMPUTING CURRENTLY TAUGHT?

No in–depth comparison between the computing courses presently delivered by colleges and universities in the United Kingdom is available. Reference to computer syllabi presented in undergraduate course brochures shows that an approach frequently adopted is to offer subjects which provide basic computing background and skills early in a course, and develop these further in later years of study. For example, introductory subjects generally expose students to spreadsheets, databases, word processing software and computer terminology. In these cases tuition frequently involves formal lectures and 'hands on' tutorials where students use these programs to solve construction related problems. Once students have completed these introductory topics they are expected to use their newly acquired skills as everyday tools in their studies. For example, they may

	Year 1	Year 2	Year 3	Year 4
Semester 1	Principles of Law Introduction to Quantity Surveying Building Materials Building Technology (Domestic Structures) Structural Analysis and Mechanics 1 Introduction to Computing	**Practical training within sponsoring companies**	Principles of Economics Health and Safety Building Services 3 Civil Engineering Technology Land and Building Law Management of Human Resources	Design and Planning Analysis and Estimation of Costs Research Dissertation Contract Administration **Options** European Language (Elementary) European Language (Advanced) Advanced Construction Construction Computing Civil Engineering Measurement
Semester 2	Construction Management Techniques Building Services 1 Site Surveying Building Production Principles of Management Technical Communication	Building Technology (Framed Structures) Building Services 2 Plant and Equipment Management Finance Building Management Measurement	**Practical training within sponsoring companies**	Maintenance, Repair and Refurbishment Research Dissertation Industrial Relations Management Information Systems Advanced Measurement Project Evaluation and Development
	Practical training (summer vacation)	**Possible additional practical training** (summer vacation)	**Practical training** (summer vacation)	**Full-time employment**

Figure A.1   The course structure of the BSc Construction Engineering Management degree

be encouraged to prepare assignments using word-processing software, and make use of spreadsheets to complete coursework for other modules.

To provide a more detailed view of one approach to the teaching of computing, the rest of this appendix provides a résumé of how this subject is taught on the BSc Construction Engineering Management (CEM) course delivered in the Department of Civil and Building Engineering at Loughborough University. This course is fully accredited by the CIOB. It is taught as a thin sandwich degree and is fully sponsored by ten major construction contractors (i.e. all students on the course are sponsored and the University receives extra funding from the sponsors to enhance the quality of teaching on the course). An overview of the current course structure is shown in Figure A.1.

The topic of computers threads its way throughout the four years of the course. Certain subjects are dedicated to the understanding and use of computers, whilst others treat computer systems as tools in the learning process. Those which deal with general computer systems and construction software not related to estimating are described in Section A.3. More detailed information on computer-aided estimating is provided in Section A.4. All descriptions are necessarily brief. Many of the subjects described here are also taken by students on the fully sponsored BSc Commercial Management and Quantity Surveying (CMQS) course which is accredited by the RICS.

A.3   GENERAL COMPUTING SUBJECTS

- *Introduction to Computing*   This is a first year subject. Its aim is to provide students with a basic understanding of computer systems and to teach them the computing skills they need during their everyday life at university. It deals with the following topics:
  - (a) *Hardware and operating systems*   A general description of computer systems; the principal components involved in a computer system; input and output devices; and common operating systems.
  - (b) *Standards*   UK, European and international computing standards and systems.
  - (c) *Computer languages*   A review of commonly used computer languages; commands, menus; general setting up and operation of personal computers.
  - (d) *Applications software*   General applications software (word processing, spreadsheets, databases).
  - (e) *CAD*   An introduction to CAD.
  - (f) *Sources of information*   Students are taught how to use library and CD-ROM databases. In addition they are introduced to the Internet, World Wide Web and electronic mail.

  Formal lectures are kept to a minimum with students spending a major part of their time in front of a computer. Emphasis is placed on students developing a degree of proficiency in using computers. The subject is assessed by means of a practical exam (again with students operating a computer) and by coursework.
- *Construction Management Techniques*   This first year subject deals mainly with statistics. Students are required to use spreadsheet software to complete some of their tutorial problems and coursework.

- *Building Production* This is also a first year subject. It deals mainly with the process of building and introduces students to planning techniques such as bar charts and network analysis. A major part involves a coursework project which requires students to plan the construction of a building. Students use planning software to produce bar charts and CAD systems for other aspects of the project.

- *Design and Planning* In their final year students prepare another coursework project based on refining the design of a building. In addition they prepare forecasts of costs and plan how the building is to be constructed. This project allows students to integrate the technical and managerial knowledge and understanding they have gained during the course, and to appreciate how this is used in the detailed design and construction planning of major buildings. They use computer systems to assist with the planning, cost estimation and presentation aspects of the project.

- *Management Information Systems* This final year subject draws together all prior learning and experience of computer systems. It introduces students to the fundamentals of Management Information Systems (MIS) and the role of these aspects within a construction company. It provides a review of current and future MIS technology and the impact of this on information systems for construction organisations. On completion, students are able to identify information system requirements and to plan, organise, and manage the implementation of new systems. The topics dealt with include:

  (a) *Concepts of information* Information management within construction organisations. A classification of information systems: business information systems; decision support systems; personal computing; office support systems; management information systems. Managers' requirements: support for planning, control, and decision making at an operational and executive level.

  (b) *MIS Technology* Hardware, software, and communications equipment. Existing software for construction management and the integration of these systems. The impact of Electronic Data Interchange (EDI), Multi-Media and Automatic Identification.

  (c) *MIS strategy* The development of an MIS strategy for an organisation. Acquiring information for systems development. Modelling information flow. Systems selection and acquisition. Implementing new systems within construction organisations.

A.4 CONSTRUCTION COMPUTING

This subject is taken by second year CMQS students as well as third and final year CEM students (for whom it is an optional subject). It provides them with a general appreciation of the computer systems available to the construction industry and first hand experience of some of the construction software currently available. The subject is mainly completed on a project basis with students working in groups simulating real construction companies. Each group aims to win a tender for the completion of a building (for example, a reinforced concrete frame of a multi-storey building such as that shown in Figure A.2) in competition with other groups. It is not necessarily the group

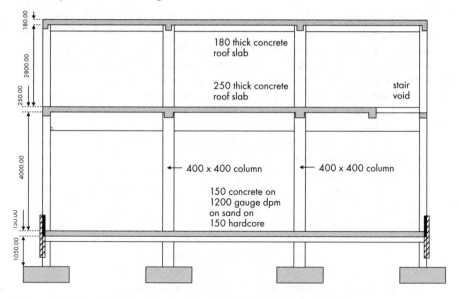

Figure A.2   Longitudinal section through reinforced concrete framed building

that submits the lowest bid that is awarded the highest marks. Other factors are also considered, such as the level of detail which students have worked to, commercial awareness and originality. Practising estimators and academic staff assess students' presentations. Rivalry between groups is intense. This subject is scheduled to allow students to relate subjects such as Building Production, Advanced Measurement and Analysis and Estimation of Costs to the software they learn about. Building Production equips students with the planning skills required to address the demands of the Construction Computing project. During Advanced Measurement students prepare a bill of quantities based on a set of construction drawings and this bill is then used in the project. Analysis and Estimation of Costs overlaps with Construction Computing and allows students to reinforce their understanding of how an estimate is prepared by requiring them to apply relevant theory during the course of their computer project.

A.4.1   What does the Construction Computing project involve?

Figure A.3 provides a diagram of the various operations involved in the project.

- *Preparing and importing bills of quantities*   At present students use word processing software to prepare bills of quantities (computer-aided bill production systems are to be used in future). This is done as one of several coursework exercises undertaken in Advanced Measurement. The bills are converted into ASCII format and then imported into a computer-aided estimating (CAE) system. This gives students first hand experience of data exchange – an aspect that is rapidly gaining importance as the construction industry moves towards the electronic interchange of data.

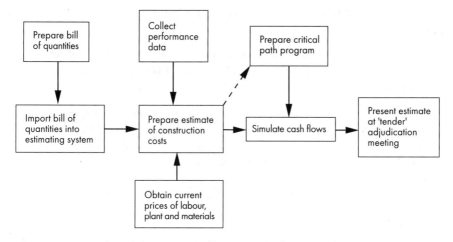

Figure A.3   The tasks completed for the Construction Computing project

- *Producing an estimate*   Students then prepare an estimate for the items of work measured in the bill of quantities. Minimal performance data are provided with the CAE software so that students have to grapple with the problems of collecting data. They develop their own classification and coding systems, select appropriate resources, assemble item build-ups, obtain materials and sub-contract costs (mostly from construction pricing manuals such as Laxton's, Spon's and Wessex pricing manuals), prepare Preliminaries costs and so on.
- *Preparing a tender construction program*   They also use a computer system to prepare a tender construction program based on critical path analysis (CPA). Resources are allocated to construction activities and students use the CPA software to level resource requirements, and to generate schedules and histograms of the resources required to construct the work. The quantities of resources arrived at using the CAE software are then compared with those calculated using the CPA software. This highlights the importance of comparing the data produced by two different systems. Students are required to explain any differences found.
- *Preparing a forecast of cash flow*   Items in the bills of quantities are then allocated to activities in the critical path network and factors affecting cash flow are entered into the computer system. Students manipulate these factors, their estimate and their construction program to obtain the most favourable cash flow they can.
- *Review meetings and presentation*   Students are required to meet several target dates at various stages of the project. At these times they consult with their tutors (and sometimes with representatives of their sponsoring companies) to review the work they have completed so far. This encourages them to work consistently throughout the project and also provides an opportunity for staff and sponsors to question their methodology, suggest alternatives and generally develop a critical analysis of their approach. The final submission of the project includes a word processed report as well as an oral presentation.

A.4.2   What are the objectives of Construction Computing and how are they assessed?

What exactly should students who have completed this subject be aware of and able to do? To assist in defining this, the following objectives have been developed over a period of several years:

- Students should have an *overall* appreciation of the major technical computer-aided applications available to the construction industry. (These include CAD, measurement, bill production, estimating, interim valuations, planning, resource smoothing, site cost control, cash flow forecasting and various other industry specific applications.)
- They should have acquired *detailed* knowledge of at least one computer-aided system for estimating, planning and cash flow forecasting and be able to use the system effectively.
- They should be able to identify and understand factors associated with the transfer of data from one application to another.

Assessment is an important aspect of any programme of study and should be related to the objectives of a subject. The methods of assessment used in Construction Computing are oral presentations, a written report (which students complete in groups) and an oral exam (completed individually). The written report counts for 80 per cent (ten per cent of which is from the various oral presentations that students complete), and the oral exam contributes twenty per cent.

Oral presentations

The main oral presentation is intended to simulate a tender adjudication meeting. Each group of students has ten to fifteen minutes to present their bid to their 'board' of directors (represented by visiting construction professionals, sponsors, academic staff and other students). All present take part in assessing the presentations. The discussion that follows each presentation is part of a wider learning experience, as students defend their estimate decisions against comments and criticism from all present. It is interesting to note that students consistently question and mark each other considerably more strictly than do construction professionals or staff!

Students are also required to meet staff (and, on occasions, their sponsors) at other oral presentations during the course of the project. These take the form of progress meetings at which students present their efforts to date. These meetings have been found to be of key importance as they highlight those areas on which students need to concentrate.

Written report

The written report (which includes all the documentation normally associated with an estimate, such as a method statement, estimate build-ups, trade summaries, a pre-tender construction programme and so on) is marked by academic staff and provides evidence of students' understanding of the subject area. It is assessed as a group project. There are several reasons for this, the most important one being to provide students with an opportunity to experience teamwork as it occurs in practice on a live estimate. Another is the obvious advantage to academic staff of reducing the workload in assessment. Students agree the distribution of marks between themselves. Several methods of ensuring that students are fairly rewarded for their efforts have been attempted over the years and this approach has been found to be the most effective one.

The written report is an essential part of assessing the project as the time allowed for the oral presentation alone is too brief to allow for in-depth assessment. Both the oral presentation and the written report give evidence of what students have achieved and their ability to operate the software.

Oral exam

At the oral exam, two members of academic staff interview each student for approximately twenty minutes. Students are questioned about the project as well as wider issues relating to the objectives of the subject. This allows staff to assess the extent to which students have understood the issues involved as well as their contribution to the work of their group. There are several benefits to this approach:

- It is felt that this is the most appropriate way of identifying the extent to which students have met the objectives of the subject (as described above).
- It serves to encourage all group members to contribute (as each is required to account for his or her efforts).
- It has proved an effective way for staff to moderate group project marks.
- Attempts at holding written exams in previous years have been problematic.

Although the task of holding oral exams for 30 plus students is demanding it is felt that the benefits of this approach warrant the effort required.

A.4.3   Student feedback

The views noted below were polled from students over the years that Construction Computing has been taught in this way. They were obtained during the formal surveys required by the University's Teaching Quality Unit and also informal discussions between staff and students.

Aspects which students enjoyed

- Being able to relate the coursework project to what actually occurs in practice.
- Using a computer system to achieve what would have been difficult and time consuming to do manually.
- Producing a cash flow 'as the effects of varying different factors were immediately obvious'.
- 'The ability of seeing one piece of coursework being used to actually have some practical and logical application/relevance.'

- Having first hand experience of how estimators build up prices.
- Working in teams.
- Several students found the adjudication simulation presentation enjoyable. Some commented that they had learnt what 'a managing director would expect to know about a tender'.

Aspects which students did NOT enjoy

- Students have complained about the timescale of the project (they effectively complete it in seven weeks). On occasions an additional week has been lost whilst students take part in an outdoor management course off campus.
- Some students found it difficult to use the system and found their lack of progress frustrating.
- Others have lost some of their work by not 'backing up' their data correctly.
- When the system was installed on our departmental computer network, some teething problems occurred and this prompted some negative remarks.
- The printing facilities provided in our department have also been criticised.
- Some students felt that the task of becoming familiar with a commercial system was too onerous.

A.4.4   Staff feedback

- *Assessment procedures*   Staff are generally satisfied with the assessment procedures used. However, one of the main difficulties has been in divorcing students' knowledge and understanding of computer systems from that of construction technology, estimating and planning. Although the criteria used in marking are explicit, staff have found themselves swayed from the objectives of the subject by students who score above or below the norm in areas other than computing. This is an on-going topic of debate and it is likely that the objectives of the subject will be modified to reflect (and thus to provide a framework for rewarding) the integrative nature of the subject.
- *Links between subjects*   Staff are pleased with the way links between Construction Computing and other subjects (such as Advanced Measurement and Analysis and Estimation of Costs) have been made. They feel that this provides an ideal opportunity to reinforce issues that students have been exposed to at various stages of their university education.
- *Commercial flair*   A desirable trait for both construction management and quantity surveying students is that they should have an appreciation of commercial pressures and opportunities. The project provided such an opportunity.
- *The cash flow exercise*   A key feature of the project is the cash flow exercise. This requires students to identify and understand links between the various aspects of preparing a tender and developing a construction programme. The effects of delaying payment to suppliers and sub-contractors, changing the sequence of construction operations, manipulating interest rates and so on are graphically illustrated by the system and were readily understood by students.

A.4.5 Evaluation of the subject – benefits to students

The views noted below were obtained during the same surveys of student views as those described in Section A.4.3.

- Students obtained a 'greater understanding of the estimating process'.
- They gained an 'insight into the use of computers in the construction industry' and 'the capabilities of construction software'.
- The project allowed students to use a computer system in a 'work' environment.
- It provided them with an understanding of how to build up an estimate and a tender.
- They were able to form a better understanding of how to estimate the costs of bill items, how to plan a construction project, the construction process, and the various aspects of predicting cash flow.
- Students viewed the project as 'a good learning experience' because they were able to see many of the topics of previous subjects put into practice.
- They felt more confident about using computer packages.

In addition staff felt that students benefited in the following ways:

- The project provided an opportunity for students to improve their communication skills.
- It allowed students to further develop skills of working in groups.
- The tight timescale of the project further simulated the commercial pressures of preparing an estimate.

A.4.6 Evaluation of the subject – benefits to staff

- As Construction Computing is run on a tutorial basis, staff have an opportunity to spend time with each student. This close contact means that less able individuals can be more readily identified and helped.
- Also as a result of this close contact, staff became aware of ambiguities in the wording of the coursework brief. This feedback would have been difficult to obtain in a traditional teaching environment.

A.4.7 Lessons learnt

- *Choice of project* Over the years several different construction projects have been used as a basis for the project. One aspect that has become apparent is that it should not be too large. Early versions of the project required students to complete an estimate for an entire bill of quantities (albeit over a longer timescale). This proved to be over-ambitious and the scale of structure shown in Figure A.2 has proved more suitable. With this project students have been required to focus on the trades of groundworks, foundations, concrete, formwork and reinforcement and foundation brickwork. Duplicating the building has made the task of scheduling resources more challenging.
- *Monitoring students* Students need to be monitored to ensure they work consistently throughout the project. The 'progress meetings' described in Section

A.4.2 have proved to be an ideal way of achieving this.

- **'Hands on' experience is essential**   Simply demonstrating software to students is of limited value. When this has been tried, students have been found to retain very little of what was shown. Actually getting students to get their hands 'dirty' has proved to be an effective way of exposing them to issues that would have not been possible otherwise.

A.4.8   Aspects still to be resolved

- **Industrial training**   At present the course is taken by third and fourth year BSc Construction Engineering Management (CEM) students and second year BSc Commercial Management and Quantity Surveying (CMQS) students. At the time that the subject is taken CEM students have been on at least one of their two six-month industrial placements, whereas the CMQS students have not yet had this opportunity. This has presented problems in the way the course has needed to be structured, with more time having to be spent discussing aspects of construction technology with those students having less site experience. Staff have manipulated the make-up of groups to encourage students to learn from their peers but the time constraints in which the project needs to be completed have hampered the success of this approach. Re-scheduling Construction Computing relative to the industrial training of CMQS students is the favoured solution.

- **Learning curve of staff**   It has taken time for staff to become familiar with the system used for the project. In addition, the intermittent way in which this subject is taught makes it difficult for them to remain conversant with the system (Construction Computing is delivered during one semester and repeated annually meaning that staff only actively use the system for approximately twelve weeks per year). This factor will undoubtedly influence any decision that needs to be made on using alternative software. Considerable staff time and effort needs to be spent in learning a system and any move to other packages will not be made lightly.

A.4.9   Choice of software

The software used for the Construction Computing project is a commercially available system. There were several reasons for choosing such a system, chief of which was the desire to make the project as realistic as possible. Once this decision had been made, staff looked for a system which transferred data between the various applications involved. This made the choice relatively straightforward as few systems allow estimated costs to be applied to the timescale defined by a critical path program and for these to then be manipulated to produce forecasts of cash flow. Notwithstanding these reasons, several other aspects are worth noting in relation to the choice of system used:

- As mentioned in Section 1.5, the market for construction software is relatively small compared to that of, for example, word processing or spreadsheet programs. CAE systems generally take longer to develop than their better selling counterparts due, in the main, to this constraint. However, this reality does little to lessen the demands of students, who understandably want to learn the latest systems. Many who are familiar with the likes of Microsoft Excel and Microsoft Word are discouraged to find that most CAE systems do not yet provide comparable functionality. Staff have found it necessary to justify their choice of software by explaining the above.

- Becoming familiar with a commercial system in a short space of time is a demanding task. The time allowed for completion of the Construction Computing project made onerous demands on students as they effectively had to complete work in seven weeks. A move to semesterisation has meant that eleven weeks are now spent on the exercise and staff feel that this extra time will alleviate this problem.
- Some of the sponsoring companies have felt that students should be exposed to the software they use in their estimating departments. Clearly a compromise has had to be reached as there are fifteen sponsors' suggestions to accommodate.

A.4.10   What now?

Computing subjects such as those described above need to evolve to keep pace with rapid developments in computer technology and demands of 'clients' (i.e. students and industry). Comments from these quarters provide staff in the Department with suggestions on ways in which the computing subjects delivered to construction managers and quantity surveyors can be improved. Aspects identified for future attention include integration with other taught modules, especially in the areas of measurement, valuations, cost control, and variations.

Flexible methods of delivering lectures and assessing performance also need to be used to cope with new approaches to solving construction problems as well as the demands of ever critical students. These approaches will continue to be used in the Department – the group work, oral and written presentations and oral exams that form part of the Construction Computing module are evidence that these objectives are being addressed.

It is too early to say whether the regime outlined above will be totally effective. This will only be possible when the performance of graduates from different courses is compared. All indications are that *using* computer programs instead of *writing* them equips students more fully to meet the challenges of the real world.

A.5   REFERENCES

Seminar unites construction education. *Construction Manager*, Vol.1, Issue 1, October 1995. ISSN 1360-3566.
Laxton's building price book. East Grinstead: Reed Information Services, ISSN 0305-6589.
Spon's architects and builders price book. London: Spon, ISSN 9235-8042.
Wessex comprehensive building price book. Poole: Wessex.

INDEX

References to specific figures and tables include the figure or table number in brackets:
figures — { }; tables — [ ].